Productivity Bargaining

A Practical Guide

R. K. Fleeman
M.I.P.M., M.B.I.M.

Chairman, Fleeman Cooper Ltd., Management Consultants,
lately Director of Personnel, Tubes Limited Group.

and

A. G. Thompson
B.Sc., M.Sc., C.Eng., M.I.C.E., M.B.I.M.

Managing Director, Productivity Consulting Services (Edinburgh) Ltd.,
Management Consultants, lately Director of Management Services,
Tubes Limited Group.

LONDON
BUTTERWORTHS
1970

ENGLAND: BUTTERWORTH & CO. (PUBLISHERS) LTD.
LONDON: 88 KINGSWAY, W.C.2

AUSTRALIA: BUTTERWORTH & CO. (AUSTRALIA) LTD.
SYDNEY: 20 LOFTUS STREET
MELBOURNE: 343 LITTLE COLLINS STREET
BRISBANE: 240 QUEEN STREET

CANADA: BUTTERWORTH & CO. (CANADA) LTD.
TORONTO: 14 CURITY AVENUE, 374

NEW ZEALAND: BUTTERWORTH & CO. (NEW ZEALAND) LTD.
WELLINGTON: 49/51 BALLANCE STREET
AUCKLAND: 35 HIGH STREET

SOUTH AFRICA: BUTTERWORTH & CO. (SOUTH AFRICA) LTD.
DURBAN: 33/35 BEACH GROVE

Standard Book Number: 406 47900 3

Printed in Great Britain at
the St Ann's Press, Park Road, Altrincham

Preface

In 1967, when we were both with Tube Investments, the proposals for a productivity agreement for the factory at Aston, Birmingham, were published. No one in T.I. had any conception at that time of the interest the proposals would arouse, although we had been aware that we were covering relatively untrodden ground. The proposals attracted attention initially because of their comprehensive nature, and subsequently because of the problems and pitfalls encountered before the agreement was signed in 1968. The proposals formed the basis of Eddie Robertson's excellent research paper on 'Productivity Bargaining and the Engineering Industry' and most of the story up to the signing of the agreement can be found there.

With the benefit of hindsight and exposure to other productivity bargains we would inevitably suggest changes if the Tubes agreement were written again today. The original proposals, however, still represent a sound approach to a productivity agreement and their use in case studies and seminars has proved their value as examples. Their inclusion in Appendix 1 is not therefore entirely accounted for by sentiment.

The Tubes agreement brought us many enquiries from other companies and requests of where to find information and guidance on productivity bargaining. There was no practical, comprehensive work which described the development of a productivity agreement and we were persuaded to write one ourselves.

We have tried to cover all the steps in the sequence they could be expected to follow in practice. Our aim has been to keep the book compact enough to appeal to the busy reader but, at the same time, to describe the various techniques in sufficient detail to show their uses and limitations. The methods given provide a sound basis from which to develop variations to suit particular applications. The contents are mainly inarguable fact but we would be less than human if our views and hobby horses did not make an occasional appearance.

Although the book is written with an industrial slant we hope it will be useful not only to the industrial executive but also to others—such as those in local government services—who are becoming increasingly aware of the benefits of productivity bargaining. We have also kept in mind the young manager and the student of management, and we hope they will find our treatment of the subject, and the descriptions of the various techniques used, particularly helpful.

Some people dislike the term Productivity *Bargain* because of its connotations of market place haggling. We have in general used 'productivity bargaining' to describe the process and 'productivity agreements' when referring to the finished article. 'Productivity bargaining' is however the generally accepted terminology and it is idle to deny that most agreements are preceded by some haggling. The difference with well constructed productivity proposals is that the haggling is informed and is within defined limits.

We wish to record our thanks to all those who have helped in the preparation of this book and we acknowledge our debt to our colleagues in Tube Investments Ltd. who stimulated our thinking and added to our experience over a number of years. Finally we thank Mr. Roy Pickering for providing the information on the Parkinson Cowan Appliances Ltd. agreement used in Appendix 1.

Birmingham   R.K.F.   A.G.T.
November 1969

Contents

		PAGE
Preface		iii
1.	INTRODUCTION TO PRODUCTIVITY BARGAINING	1
2.	MEASUREMENT OF THE WORKER'S CONTRIBUTION —MEASUREMENT OF WORK AND PRODUCTIVITY	10
3.	MANAGEMENT'S CONTRIBUTION TO PRODUCTIVITY IMPROVEMENT	29
4.	JOB EVALUATION AND WAGES STRUCTURE..	41
5.	PREPARING FOR PRODUCTIVITY BARGAINING	63
6.	PREPARATION OF THE SURVEY AND DEVELOPING THE WAGES STRUCTURE..	81
7.	FORMULATING, NEGOTIATING AND IMPLEMENTING THE PRODUCTIVITY BARGAIN	88
8.	MONITORING, REVIEWING AND DEVELOPING THE PRODUCTIVITY AGREEMENT	104
	Appendix 1 Examples of Productivity Agreement Proposals	109
	Appendix 2 Profile of Contributions to Productivity	119
	Appendix 3 Management Surveys	122
	Appendix 4 Attitude Surveys	124
	Appendix 5 Example of Formal Communications Structure	126
	Appendix 6 Use of Computers in Productivity Bargaining	128
	Appendix 7 Guidelines for Efficiency Agreements Including Productivity Agreements	130
	BIBLIOGRAPHY	133
	INDEX	135

1

Introduction to Productivity Bargaining

To most people, a productivity agreement was until recently, synonomous with Fawley and Esso. At this refinery for a very substantial increase in basic wages of about 40 per cent, overtime was reduced from 18 per cent in 1960 to between 4 and 11 per cent in 1962. There was also a reduction in craftsmen's mates and of the need to use outside contractors. This was a splendid but isolated example of what could be done, and it was contrasted at the time with evidence that Britain was operating at half-time effort for half-time pay. Comparisons showed, and show today if they are made again, that the average U.S. worker generates two or more times as much wealth for his company as does his British counterpart and earns correspondingly more.

This outstanding example at Fawley which was documented by Alan Flanders and widely publicized, did not attract many imitators. The firm of consultants which had been employed at Fawley went on to the Rootes factory at Linwood in Scotland. Here, there was not the same ambience that existed at Fawley. Contraction of output occurred at the critical time and from much effort, little was achieved.

The same consultants assisted Alcan Industries Ltd. to negotiate a Productivity Agreement in 1964–65. Eventually, in 1966, productivity increases of over 10 per cent were visible with a considerable drop in overtime.

At about the same time, the Gases Division of the British Oxygen Company introduced an agreement which reduced hours of work from 52 to 44 with no increase in the wages bill and no loss of output.

Most of the early agreements were concerned with reducing overtime and with providing more flexible arrangements for organizing manpower. Also, the industries concerned were mostly process industries—oil refineries, chemical plants, distribution etc. and the role of the direct production worker in the agreement was often secondary to that of the maintenance workers. Nevertheless, the idea of a statesmanlike agreement in which a great many restrictive practices were exchanged for substantial increases in wages was a useful one.

The National Board for Prices and Incomes soon after its inception, gave support to productivity agreements. In one way and another, the

1

activity gained momentum and became known, unofficially, as productivity bargains or productivity deals. Some of the Employers' Associations began to look more favourably on these localized agreements. A start was made in introducing the principles of the productivity bargain into manufacturing industry. An early example of this type was concluded at Tubes Ltd., Birmingham, and this is described more fully in Appendix I.

The Donovan report also gave its blessing and it is now apparent that something new in the field of productivity and industrial relations has arrived. Productivity bargaining is still a tyro with much further scope for development. It can already be seen as a unifying influence between management and labour and as a part of the 'total' concept of the firm, along with corporate planning, management-by-results and the rest.

WHAT IS PRODUCTIVITY BARGAINING?

What is generally meant by productivity bargaining is an agreement between the management of an enterprise and its employees which has certain characteristics:

i. it is a local agreement relating to one enterprise in one location;

ii. it is usually comprehensive in scope, combining as far as possible, all that management wants from its employees in return for all that the employees want from management. The intention is that it should be in the nature of a settlement of all outstanding grievances and difficulties in order to eliminate most, if not all, inhibitions and restrictions to increasing the productivity and prosperity of the firm;

iii. it is a bargain, i.e. a negotiated series of concessions and gains on the workers' side set against concessions and gains on the management side, and it is based fundamentally on improvements in productivity.

iv. it should be constructed in such a way that each part of the bargain is honoured by ensuring that gains and concessions are progressively linked.

The Prices & Incomes Board have listed guide lines which productivity bargains should follow. These are given fully in Appendix 7 but may be summarized as follows:

1. Workers should make a direct contribution.
2. Forecasts of productivity should be soundly based.
3. Total cost per unit of output should be reduced.
4. Extra payment should only be made for increased productivity.
5. The company should make a contribution to stable prices.

6. The overall cost throughout the company of the productivity agreement should be taken into account in (3) above.
7. Extravagant levels of pay which would provoke resentment elsewhere should be avoided. Additionally both employers and unions are responsible for seeing that proper controls are included.

Various factors have contributed to the growth of this type of management/worker agreement. One of these has been the growing realization that industry-wide collective agreements have declined in effectiveness. So often national agreements on pay are rendered little more than academic by local payment-by-results systems, additions to rates, and overtime pay. Another reason has been the decline in authority of both Employers' Associations and Trade Unions.

One cannot do better than quote from the Royal Commission on Trade Unions and Employers' Associations 1965–1968.

Para. 1019. The central defect in British industrial relations is the disorder in factory and workshop relations and pay structures promoted by the conflict between the formal and the informal systems. To remedy this, effective and orderly collective bargaining is required over such issues as the control of incentive schemes, the regulation of hours actually worked, the use of job evaluation, work practices and the linking of changes in pay to changes in performance, facilities for shop stewards and disciplinary rules and appeals. In most industries such matters cannot be dealt with effectively by means of industry-wide agreements.

Para. 1020. Factory-wide agreements can however provide the remedy. Factory agreements (with company agreements as an alternative in multi-plant companies) can regulate actual pay, constitute a factory negotiating committee and grievance procedures which suit the circumstances, deal with such subjects as redundancy and discipline and cover the rights and obligations of shop stewards. A factory agreement can assist competent managers, many current industry-wide agreements have become a hindrance to them.

DEVELOPING THE BARGAIN

Before a productivity bargain can be constructed it is necessary to investigate, list, and evaluate:
1. what the workers want from management.
2. what the workers can give to management.
These are the components from which a bargain is constructed.

WHAT THE WORKERS WANT

It is usually assumed that workers generally want increased wages. This is true, but many other factors can be important. Security of employment is often high on the workers' list. It is difficult always to ensure this if productivity is increased in a firm which cannot increase its sales. Workers also wish to have a simple wages structure which they can readily understand and which provides stable earnings. Holidays, canteens, lavatories, car parking facilities, transport, communication structures are examples of other factors which workers might regard as important. The possibilities are many and it is vital to ensure that all the important ones in any particular firm, are known. It is necessary to seek the views of management, particularly supervision, and of the workers themselves. This may be done by questionnaires and interviews conducted on a sampling basis. The problem of knowing what the workers want becomes more difficult as the size of the firm increases. The need for surveys of attitudes and aspirations to become more formalized correspondingly increases.

WHAT THE WORKERS CAN GIVE

Management often know some of the things which they wish to obtain from workers. It is rare for them to know everything that could be conceded which would benefit the firm and which the workers would be prepared to offer, and a careful investigation by interview and questionnaire will often be needed.

The most frequently occurring difficulties are concerned with shift work and demarcations, and with timekeeping and absenteeism. The working of new equipment with a minimum number of operators is another objective which management is often trying to achieve.

MATCHING THE NEEDS AND POTENTIAL CONTRIBUTIONS OF WORKERS AND MANAGEMENT

The productivity bargain is, by definition above, comprehensive and usually takes months or possibly a year or so to implement. Thus, concessions on one side cannot always be immediately compensated for by corresponding gains.

The standard situation is where management offer a simplified and rationalized wages structure as a first stage. This generally costs the firm money and it is not always possible to find sufficiently valuable concessions from the workers to compensate. However, this first stage may be offered, for example, on condition that incentive schemes are re-assessed by work measurement in the second stage. Some form of interim award may also be demanded. Management in this situation have to pay out a good deal of money in order to secure future benefits.

If the management survey of the potential contributions of the workers has been thorough, it may be possible to match concessions and gains more closely over the implementation period of the bargain.

WORKING OUT THE FINANCIAL ASPECTS

There are three elements involved in the basic financial considerations for the Company:

    i. the fixed costs of the bargain.
    ii. the costs which vary with productivity.
    iii. the benefits of increased productivity.

The fixed costs include the costs of job evaluation, rationalizing the wages structure, internal staff costs, consultant's fees, consequential increases and interim awards. If part of the bargain is to introduce shifts, then this will cost extra in shift allowances and there will be the cost of extra staff to supervise the shifts. These costs may be offset by reductions in overtime and in numbers of workers. As with most capital expenditures, it is all too easy to underestimate or insufficiently allow for all that is involved.

The costs which vary with productivity are the bonus payments and any other payments that may be linked, such as supervisors' salaries.

The value of increased productivity depends largely on whether the increase in factory capacity so created can be utilized profitably. If it cannot, then the value of the increased productivity will appear as reductions in numbers of people employed. The bargain will be much more attractive to the management if there is an unsatisfied demand for its products, so that the increased output can be sold. There may be other benefits such as savings in production materials or consumables which immediately accrue to the company.

This financial situation can be represented as in Fig. 1. It is similar to the usual break-even chart but with benefits to the Company replacing sales. For there to be a break-even point at all, the benefit of the increased productivity resulting from incentive must be greater than the cost of the incentive. The higher the fixed cost, the less the scope for paying a substantial incentive bonus. Yet it is often this bonus which management depends upon to get the benefits needed to pay for the bargain. This is a key point and is a warning to management to avoid conceding too much unilaterally in the early stages of a negotiation.

A productivity bargain is often a major capital investment with a substantial initial outlay from which a return is expected in the future. It is therefore appropriate to apply the techniques of capital investment appraisal. Discounted cash flow calculations will show that the sooner the returns are obtained, the more attractive will the investment be. Delays in carrying out work measurement or productivity measurement and implementing the part of the bargain which brings the substantial benefits to the company are costly. For example, a bargain that costs £50,000 initially and which reaches the break-even point in twelve months (*see* Fig. 1) and saves £30,000 p.a. thereafter, will have recouped its overall cost in about three years. If the break-even points takes twenty-four months to be attained, it will take six years or more to recoup the overall cost. The difference in timing will be worth £50,000 or so. Hence, it would be worth while spending at least £20,000 or so on outside assistance to get the bargain implemented as quickly as possible.

Assessment of cost must also take account of the cost of not implementing a productivity bargain. This will at least be the cost of some wage increases but may be the cost of an inability to recruit scarce labour or the cost of worsening labour relations.

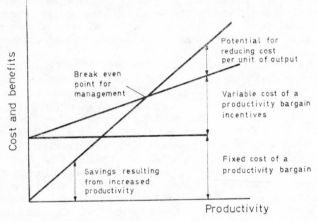

Fig. 1

COSTS AND BENEFITS OF A PRODUCTIVITY BARGAIN

The gains from the workers' point of view are generally simpler to estimate. Nevertheless there are a number of factors to be considered. The gross wage may not be greatly increased in some instances due to the reduction in overtime hours. The value of increased leisure time has to be assessed. The rate at which new or revised bonus schemes are introduced affect the workers' return as well as that of management. The effect of inflation and the renunciation of alternative wage claims are also factors for the workers' to consider.

The gain to the community at large must substantially stem from the real increased purchasing power of the workers. There may be subsidiary benefits in terms of reduced selling prices or static selling prices in an inflationary era. Benefits might also take the form of increased exports as a result of increased capacity. Overall, the gain should be the move towards a higher paid (in real terms) and more productive work force.

COMPANY-WIDE IMPLICATIONS OF PRODUCTIVITY BARGAINING

Aspects discussed so far have indicated the comprehensiveness of productivity bargaining. The potential effects can extend very far within the firm as well as over a considerable period of time. Further consideration is given in Chapter 2 to the variety of sustained contributions that can be made by the workers. These include not only working harder and more effectively, but saving materials and consumables, helping to eliminate idle time, and helping to achieve on-time deliveries, and so on.

The supply of labour is something which requires careful planning. Increasingly it is a scarce resource. Medium- to long-range planning should indicate the quantity and type of labour resources required by a firm over the succeeding five to ten years. Targets of productivity and of worker contributions to the prosperity of the firm can also properly be derived from corporate planning exercises. The objectives of a productivity bargain should stem, therefore, from the future needs of the company and the bargain should be designed to fulfil these objectives as far as possible. Where careful investigation demonstrates the impossibility of achieving desirable objectives arising from Long-Range Planning, then it is necessary to feed back the realistic expectations to the Long-Range Plan.

The productivity bargain is therefore seen to be generally company-wide and to be part of the life of the company over a period of time. There are situations where a Sectional Bargain may be appropriate and these are discussed in Chapter 7. Long-Range Planning, properly carried out, will take account of changes expected in social organization and in technology. Such considerations may well affect the shape of a productivity bargain if it is expected to last for a number of years. The bargain should not be a static once-and-for-all settlement, but should lead somewhere—to a developing understanding and communication between workers and managers. It might be that a company would have as a long-term objective, profit sharing or co-partnership or some other method of integrating workers more closely into the life of the firm. If this were so, then the productivity bargain should generate movement in the desired direction.

COMMUNICATION

An essential part of a productivity bargain is the improvement of communication between workers and management. For this to work, it is necessary for the instruments of communication—the channels and committees, etc.—to be concerned with real and important matters. The objective should be to move away from the emotional and intellectual set pieces, towards greater realism. Another necessary condition of good communication is mutual understanding and tolerance—a two-way flow of these scarce but cultivatable characteristics.

THE PARTIES INVOLVED IN A PRODUCTIVITY AGREEMENT

1. *The workers* are represented within the firm by shop stewards. Outside the firm, are the *full-time Union officials* who are concerned with ensuring that arrangements within the firm are in line with union policy. This is already a complicated social organization with three separate components who have to communicate with each other. In any firm, there will often be several Unions so that there are additional complications of communications between Unions at the three levels and the possibility of conflicting interests.

2. *The management* is not as homogeneous as it looks. Clearly, the main outlines and policies of a productivity bargain must be endorsed by the chief executive, e.g. Managing Director, and by the other senior executives of the company. Supervision is in direct contact with the workers and must be consulted at all stages. Some senior members of management will be responsible for the productivity bargain as a whole. Personnel, Work Study, and other functional managers will also be involved. Again, problems of communication within this group have to be solved adequately. Over the period of construction, negotiation and implementation of a bargain, changes in management at all levels may occur and positive action has to be taken to ensure continuity—particularly of enthusiasm and commitment.

3. *Consultants* are often retained by management to assist in the preparation and implementation of productivity bargains. It is important that the company management provides them with clear Terms of Reference and defines their function in the activity.

4. *Employers' Associations* are increasingly making arrangements to provide their member firms with information and assistance on productivity bargaining. This is another party that has to be kept in mind and informed.

5. *Government*—the Department of Employment and Productivity will wish to be informed of the proposed bargain. The Prices and Incomes Board is also in the background and a particular settlement may be referred. It is necessary therefore for those concerned with productivity bargaining to have regard to the P.I.B. guidelines.

Leadership in arranging the necessary communication and consultation between all these interested parties devolves upon management —usually Senior Management.

THE MAIN STEPS IN PRODUCTIVITY BARGAINING

The starting point is generally a realization that ad hoc responses to wage and other demands generally result in higher labour costs per unit of output. There is also the realization that the utilization of the company's resources—machines, materials, consumables, etc.—by the workers could be greatly improved. The potential value of this is so great that settlement of many issues between workers and management becomes financially possible.

The next steps involve discovering the main components of a bargain —the workers' and management's concessions and gains, and the basis of motivation that will ensure that pay increases are linked effectively to changes in productivity. This leads to consideration of the measurement of present levels of productivity and of how productivity may be measured in the future.

It is desirable to understand the company-wide potential for cost reduction and productivity improvement, assuming optimum motivation of workers and management alike, separately and in co-operation. Some assessment of likely gains in financial terms is required. This is a technical field in which statistical analysis and computers have an important part to play.

Rationalization and simplification of the wages structure is frequently required. A prerequisite is a review of all jobs, preparation of job descriptions, and implementation of job evaluation. A wide variety of possible wage structures is possible and computer simulation can assist in evaluating the effect of different proposals.

Consideration of the above factors allows an outline productivity bargain to be prepared. Some companies have considered it useful to establish an agreed list of principles as a 'Statement of Intent' with the workers' representatives. In any event, it is necessary for management to have a well thought out set of propositions as a starting point for negotiations. These should be thoroughly understood by all levels of management before they are put before the workers' representatives.

From this stage, negotiations begin and in due course a productivity bargain will be agreed. This then has to be implemented together with adequate consultation and communication structures. Monitoring and administrative systems have also to be developed and implemented and the progress of the bargain should be reviewed at regular intervals.

In larger companies it is useful to develop arrow diagrams and to identify the critical path. These may be up-dated manually, or by computer if the complexity justifies it. Productivity bargaining is a complex activity which makes heavy demands on the organizing abilities of a company.

Nevertheless, productivity bargaining offers the opportunity to workers and management in an enterprise to make a fresh start. Measured in terms of days lost in strikes, the British record, though not a cause for congratulation, compares favourably with that of many other countries. Measured in terms of liberating the co-operative and creative energies of its total work force as reflected in national statistics of productivity growth, there is a considerable challenge to be faced.

2

Measurement of the Worker's Contribution—Measurement of Work and Productivity

INTRODUCTION—ECONOMICS AND CONTRIBUTIONS

The basic economics involved in most firms can be illustrated as in Fig. 2.

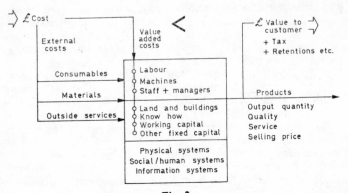

Fig. 2

BASIC ECONOMICS OF A FIRM

The objective from the firm's point of view is to get the maximum output from each input of wages, capital, machines, management, production materials and consumables. The worker can clearly make contributions to this process in various ways. Not only can he directly affect output but he can also influence the effectiveness with which the other inputs are used.

Working on his own or within a small group or team, the worker can assist in obtaining a higher volume of good output by his individual performance, i.e. working harder, faster, or more effectively. He can also assist the other members of the group and/or use a machine more effectively to produce more output. Yet again, he can influence the quality of output so that only good work is produced or allowed to go forward to the next process. The worker is also part of a larger group: the department in which he works.

In relation to obtaining maximum output from all the resources employed, the individual worker can make a number of contributions in order to:

i. ensure a better use of the total labour resources, e.g. a machine operator may assist a maintenance operative when his machine is broken down.
ii. avoid waste of production materials.
iii. ensure maximum output from all machines in the department.
iv. obtain maximum overall output.
v. ensure work is completed on time.
vi. ensure best utilization of all consumables.

Finally, the worker is part of the firm as a whole and again can make the contributions i.–vi. listed above to the overall prosperity of the firm.

CATEGORIES OF EMPLOYEES:

The main groups involved in a firm may be listed as:

1. direct production workers.
2. indirect production workers.
3. skilled service workers (often belonging to craft unions).
4. staff workers.
5. supervision.
6. management.

Direct production workers are frequently classified as being those workers who directly alter the shape or condition of the product. From the point of view of productivity measurement, it is more useful to consider direct production workers as those workers, the effect of whose effort and skill can be directly measured by work measurement techniques.

Indirect production workers can then be considered to be those who assist direct production workers but the effect of whose effort and skill cannot be directly measured by work measurement techniques. A cranedriver is an example of such a worker.

The work of *skilled service workers* is generally characterized as being of considerable variety and variability as to work content. Some of their work can be directly measured by work measurement. The remainder of their work is then assessed in some way. Maintenance work is the most common example of this type of activity.

The work of *staff* may be concerned with clerical operations, technical work, draughting, computer work and so on. In most firms, about 80 per cent of this work can be measured by work measurement techniques. There remains a residue of jobs such as that of telephone operators, gate-keepers, etc. who do whatever work comes forward for them to do. In this respect they are similar to some indirect production workers.

B

COMPANY...

PROFILE   O F   C O N T R I B U T I O N S

SCORING: 1 — INSIGNIFICANT, 2 — SIGNIFICANT,

MARK $\boxed{A}$ -- PRESENT POSITION

ASSESSOR...

Type of Contribution	Higher Output of Machine or Small Group			Higher Labour Productivity of Department				
Category of Worker	Individual Performance	Machine or Small Group - Output/Hour	Quality of Output	Labour Productivity	Material Productivity	Machine Productivity	Output	Delivery Performance
DIRECT PRODUCTION								
INDIRECT PRODUCTION								
MAINTENANCE & CRAFT								
CLERICAL								
SUPERVISION								
MIDDLE-MANAGEMENT								

PROFILE OF CONTRIBUTIONS TO PRODUCTIVITY   *Fig. 3*

DEPARTMENT...

| T O   P R O D U C T I V I T Y |

3 – FAIRLY IMPORTANT, 4 – IMPORTANT, 5 – VERY IMPORTANT

/B/ – POTENTIAL POSITION

DATE...

Greater Prosperity Opportunities of the Firm										
Labour Productivity	Material Productivity	Machine Productivity	Consumables Productivity	Output	Delivery Performance					

The efficacy of *supervision* is in part reflected by the performance of those they supervise, but their work cannot be directly measured. The same applies to various levels of *management*. Techniques of Management by Objectives are appropriate to supervision and management. If these are in use, there should be co-ordination with the objectives of the productivity bargain.

PATTERN OF POTENTIAL CONTRIBUTIONS

Each category of employee will have some level of influence on each of the three objectives involved in productivity bargaining, namely: higher output of the individual, small group or machine; higher labour productivity of the department; greater prosperity opportunities for the firm. This situation may be summarized as shown in Fig. 3. A profile for any particular company may be derived by putting a score in each cell to reflect the effect each category of worker has on each contribution. The basis of scoring is indicated on the form. This is done in the top triangle in each cell. In the bottom triangle is scored the desirable and attainable contribution.

An example, with an interpretation of the use of the profile in developing a productivity bargain is given in Appendix 2.

From this general picture, the objective in the remainder of this chapter is to concentrate on the contributions of direct, indirect, and skilled service workers and how these can be measured.

The performance of individual direct production workers is measured by a variety of work measurement techniques. The performance of a group of workers in terms of their effectiveness in obtaining output from a machine may require a modification to the work measurement technique—or a different technique altogether. The assessment of the effectiveness of the contributions of large groups of workers in a department or factory involves the technique popularly known as productivity measurement. Finally, the measurement of overall prosperity and assessment of workers' contributions to this involve conceptions of added value.

WORK MEASUREMENT—MEASUREMENT OF INDIVIDUAL AND SMALL GROUP EFFORT AND EFFECTIVENESS

The objective of work measurement can be considered to be either the measurement of the performance of a worker or a means of assessing how much time should be taken to complete a specified job.

When a single worker on his own is involved, the time to do the job and the work performance are directly related. Where several workers are involved, the relationship between individual performance and time to complete the job is more complicated and depends on the way the individuals in the team work together. Where, further, a machine is involved, the relationship becomes even more complex by virtue of machine speeds and feeds, and other features of the technology of the process.

Where it is desired to reward each individual worker in accordance with his own effort, the emphasis of the work measurement technique is on the individual. The monitoring of performance will tend to be in terms of the individual rather than in terms of the output of the work group and/or machine. On the other hand, the interest of the firm is fundamentally in the productivity of the work group, i.e. the amount of work obtained from the work group in relation to the number of people and the time involved. If the amount of work can be measured in physical terms, week by week, then productivity *can* be expressed as so much output per work group or machine time. However, where the output is not measurable in this way, it is necessary to think in terms of a standard cycle or floor-to-floor time.

In practice, a relationship between individual performance and the output of the work group is developed to assist the workers involved. They can only judge their performance in terms of the actual output they produce.

In the most frequently used method of work measurement, each job is defined and specified. The time to do the job is measured, often using a stop-watch.

What is normally meant by work measurement should perhaps more accurately be called element time study. This is because of the technique which is used of dividing a job into a number of sequential intervals of time corresponding to definite stages in the carrying out of the job. These are called elements.

The reason for dividing the job into elements is so that each element of work can be studied in detail. Studies can also be made to see how the elements can be combined, eliminated, or carried out simultaneously. Further, if enough jobs are studied, it is found that the same elements repeat. In theory, it is then not necessary to time these elements. Eventually, there may be a sufficient library of elements to make it unnecessary to time a job at all. It can be built up—synthesized, from previously measured elements. This technique is known as using synthetics. In practice, it is surprising that so little advantage is taken of the opportunity to use synthetics, and job after job is often studied element by element in its entirety. Normally, the length of an element is between eight and thirty seconds.

RATING

The principle of rating is based on the principle of assigning a scale of numbers to represent different rates of working. One scale which was very popular but is gradually going out of use represents the number 60 as the rate of working of a production worker with no financial incentive and 80 as that of a production worker with a financial incentive, i.e. a piecework rate of working. An attempt to give more objective reality to the idea of a rate of working is to define the 80 rate as that 'which an average man, suited and accustomed to his task, can maintain throughout his normal working period apart from the necessary time taken for rest, without at the end of that period being more than normally, healthily tired'. Rating films are available in which workers are to be seen carrying out various operations—at a different rate of working in each scene. These films can be shown to the time study observers who estimate (i.e. rate) the rate of working of the workmen in the film. At the end of the film or a series of films, the observer's rates are compared with the 'correct' rating and the observer is informed of his error. In this way he can adjust his ideas to approximate more closely to the standard.

The purpose of rating is to convert all observed times to a standard rate of working. For example, an element of work (A) was timed as taking nine seconds to complete and the rate of working was assessed as 40 (on the 0–60–80 etc. scale). For another element (B), the time was twelve seconds and the rating 70.

If the standard rate of working is 60, then the times can be converted to this standard as follows:

Element (A)—time at 60 rate$= 9 \times \frac{40}{60} = 6$ seconds
Element (B)—time at 60 rate$=12 \times \frac{70}{60} =14$ seconds.

This is the way the time study observer overcomes the problem of timing slow and fast workers and establishes a time at standard rate of working.

There are three rating scales in common use and they are illustrated in Fig. 4.

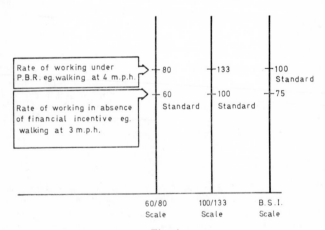

Fig. 4

COMPARISON OF RATING SCALES

REST ALLOWANCES

The time that should be allowed to do a job depends not only on the rate of working, but also on the nature of the work, because it is not reasonable to expect a worker to work all day without rest, and the amount of rest he will require will depend upon a number of factors. These include the amount of effort (mental and physical) required, and the amount of noise, heat, humidity and discomfort involved. The exact allowance to make for any given set of conditions is again a subjective judgement, but tables giving guidance on the appropriate rest allowances are generally used to reduce inconsistency.

Some rest must be allowed for any job however easy it is to carry out. When a worker is using a machine or is part of a team, there may be periods of time during the work cycle when he has nothing to do and it can therefore be assumed that he is resting during this time. But apart from this, some part of the rest allowance must assume that the worker can leave his work place for his own personal needs. In practice in this type of situation, some of the rest allowance is reckoned as taking place during the work cycle and some outside the work cycle, and only the percentage attributable to the rest taken outside the work cycle is used as a rest allowance.

STANDARD TIME

A normalized time to which the appropriate rest allowance has been added is a standard time. It is measured in minutes but it is not really a measure of time but rather a measure of a certain amount of work—the amount of work that an average worker performing at standard rate and taking the appropriate rest allowance would carry out in one clock minute. Such a minute is known as a standard minute, and whatever the scale, 60 standard minutes of work are performed every hour by workers working at standard rates and taking standard rest allowances. Sometimes standard minutes (S.Ms.) are called work units.

The Standard Time is the time issued to the worker. On the British Standard Scale it represents a target time which should be attainable with reasonable effort and application. On some other scales, it represents an easy time which can readily be beaten, and is thus rather more acceptable to the worker, in the psychological sense.

CONTINGENCIES

Most jobs consist of a series of elements (i.e. a series of happenings) which occur every time the job is done. There are also generally a number of happenings which occur occasionally. This situation is dealt with by finding the standard time for each of these contingencies and also the frequency of occurrence. Each standard time is then divided by the average number of routine cycles between each occurrence of the contingency. This fraction of the contingency standard time is then added to the standard time for the routine part of the job.

PERFORMANCE

The term 'performance' used in work measurement is synonomous with productivity. It is the output—measured as standard minutes—divided by the input—measured as clock minutes. Performance can be measured and stated for an individual, small group or department. Standard performance is 60 on the 60/80 scale, 100 on the 100/133 scale but 100 on the British Standard 75/100 scale.

SUMMARY—ELEMENT TIME STUDY

The steps involved in setting a standard time by element time study are:

    (a) Select the work to be measured.
    (b) Record all relevant data.
    (c) Break the job down into elements.
    (d) Time and rate the elements.
    (e) Normalize the elements.
    (f) Add rest allowance.
    (g) Add effect of contingencies.
    (h) Obtain standard minute value of work content.

The accuracy of standards devised from time study has been the subject of considerable research. Considering the variability of jobs themselves and the subjective factors involved, the accuracy of individual estimates of job times is probably not great, e.g. ± 10 per cent to ± 20 per cent. It is likely therefore that too much effort is spent in work study departments in seeking an ideal accuracy which will never be attained. Much saving of effort can result from a more statistically minded approach, with relationships expressed in simple form and with values expressed to a significance appropriate to their accuracy. Such an approach has been called Standard Minute Regression Analysis.

STANDARD MINUTE REGRESSION ANALYSIS (SMRA)

SMRA relates the time of a job with the most important variables affecting it and uses the techniques of mathematical statistics. Production jobs involve one or more workers who carry out operations, for example, upon some material or component. In going through the operation, the material or component is generally altered in some way and the quantity of materials or components processed in a given time can be considered to be the output of the work-place.

The requirement is to assess a fair, standard time for completion of a job measured in terms of the quantity of materials or components processed.

SMRA is concerned with the complete cycle or floor-to-floor time, not with elements of time. Times are measured by stop watch or wrist watch. Rating and rest allowances are applied as appropriate. Other variables are measured which are likely to affect the relation betwen time and output. After a number of observations have been taken, this relation is examined, using statistical techniques, and the effect of the variables assessed. Examination at this stage enables the measurement of unimportant variables to be discontinued. It also enables an estimate to be made of the further number of time studies required to achieve a predetermined level of accuracy. In some applications, it can be shown that the time to complete a job is partly affected by the effort and effectiveness of the worker and partly by the management. These effects can be separated.

The advantage of this approach is that an assessment is made of the accuracy of standards. It utilizes data in the most effective way and reduces time study costs. The final result is also in the form most suitable for computerized pay-roll, and consists of a formula relating the floor-to-floor or cycle time with various relevent measures of output and variables.

ACTIVITY SAMPLING

Activity sampling is used as a rapid and relatively economical way of measuring the duration and characteristics of a number of activities. In developing a productivity bargain a company needs to assess the extent to which indirect workers, maintenance workers, and staff are gainfully employed.

The principle may best be explained by an example. A department has twelve fork-lift truck drivers and it is required to assess whether this is the right number.

Observations, probably several hundred, are made at random intervals of time over a number of days. Care is taken to sample all conditions, e.g. nightshift as well as dayshift, overtime periods, the beginning and end of a shift as well as the middle of a shift, etc.

In the example used here, it is necessary to know the amount of time each day that a driver and truck is idle. The amount of time machines are waiting for the driver and truck is also important and this may be found from machine operators' logs. If it is found that the trucks are idle 50 per cent of the time, then a reduction might be made from twelve to eight drivers and trucks. It would probably be wrong to reduce the number to six because this could cause excessive waiting time at machines.

SERVICE LABOUR PLANNING AND CONTROL

There is generally little information in most companies about the work of indirects, service workers, clerical staff and similar people. Many labourers, mates, truck drivers and so on are provided as a service, frequently without supervision of their own. Clerical supervisors often spend much of their time doing actual clerical work themselves. In consequence the complement of indirect workers for a particular service role is often derived from experience or hunch. It may be such that the service workers cannot achieve high performance because there are too many of them.

Scheduling is based on knowing:

    i. how long jobs take to do.

   ii. how many jobs are required to be done within a certain period.

  iii. the 'capacity' to do the required job within a certain period.

This information enables the number of workers required to provide a service to be assessed (from knowledge of the jobs involved, the frequency of their occurrence and the time to complete them).

With this approach, the principle is to vary complements of service workers to provide a full work load. In the short run this involves switching service workers from one job or location to another. This requires flexibility and training to ensure that these workers can do a variety of jobs. It also necessitates the appointment of a supervisor to utilize the total service or indirect labour force to best advantage.

A number of variants of this approach exist—in some, the times to do a job are measured by stop watch, others make assessment of batches of work using a wall clock or by using pre-determined times. Most systems have fairly elaborate systems of allocating work, measuring and reporting the work done, monitoring back logs and summarizing performances.

The techniques are only a translation into other fields of what has for many years been used in the production areas and there called production planning and control. The author has for some years referred to this technique in the clerical areas as clerical planning and control. It is equally appropriate to refer to maintenance planning and control, drawing office planning and control, laboratory planning and control and so on.

PRE-DETERMINED MOTION TIME SYSTEMS (PMTS)

A criticism of time study is that it depends on the subjective judgement of the man with the stop watch. Various efforts have been made to eliminate this subjectivity and some of these have given rise to families of systems based on pre-determined motion times.

The basis of these systems is that most elements of work can be sub-divided into a finite set of motions. This was discovered by detailed study of many films taken of various people doing various jobs. Tables are available of the times for various motions and examples are described in some of the references given at the end of this chapter.

To establish an element time, it is necessary to identify and specify each of the separate motions which go to make up the element. Once this is done, the times to accomplish the motions can be looked up in the Tables and added together to provide the element time. The element times can then be summed to provide a total time for the job, in a similar way to that in which synthetics are used in normal work measurement. This total time may not be the same as the standard time found by actual stop-watch time study and it may be necessary to apply a factor to all PMTS values. Rest and other allowances can then be added to provide the standard time for the job.

The value of PMTS is that it provides universal standards and eliminates some, at any rate, of the human element. It does focus attention on the detailed method and may allow improvements to be developed. It is also useful where it is not possible to time directly due, for example, to the workers' objections to the stop-watch.

There are some thirty systems presently available and they are frequently presented in three versions. These are:

(a) a detailed version, which is appropriate to examining manual operations in detail often with the aid of cine-photography,

(b) a simplified version, appropriate for use with short-cycle work which does not require photographic methods. As this process still takes a considerable time it is only economic to use with repetitive processes,

(c) a considerably simplified version, appropriate to longer-cycle work.

The best known of these schemes is MTM (Motion Time Measurement) and Work Factor.

STANDARD DATA

There are a large number of jobs which occur over and over again not only in a particular factory, but throughout the industrial and commercial world. These include such jobs as opening envelopes, sweeping floors, etc. For most of these, standard times have been established and are available in various forms.

The use of such standard times can save much effort and can also provide a basis for checking against time standard values.

ESTIMATED TIMES AND BENCH-MARKS

Sometimes, when time study is not possible (some Trade Unions still refuse to accept it), and the use of PMTS would be too laborious, times are estimated by skilled estimators. They analyse the job into a series of steps or elements and estimate the time for each element.

This has been termed Analytical Estimating and is based on the idea that it is more accurate to break a job down into a number of parts and estimate these separately, than to estimate a time for the job as a whole. An alternative to analytical estimating is to establish as accurately as possible and with considerable care and effort, the time to complete a series of well-known established jobs. (PMTS systems are sometimes useful for doing this.) The jobs are also chosen in accordance with the length of time they take to complete, so as to produce a series of successively longer taking jobs covering the range of completion times for all jobs likely to have to be estimated. Having established these bench-mark jobs (taking $\frac{1}{4}$ hour, $\frac{1}{2}$ hour, 1 hour, $1\frac{1}{2}$ hours, etc.) then all other jobs are assessed as to which benchmark job they most closely resemble. When this is found, then the bench-mark time is assigned to the new job.

RECAPITULATION

The end result of work measurement is to establish tables or formulae which provide standard times for the completion of defined jobs. In assessing a worker's performance for a particular period, the work measured standards are used to derive the total standard time from knowledge of the quantity of actual jobs done. This will generally be expressed as standard minutes. The workers' performance is then expressed as the ratio of standard to actual clock minutes in the period.

The commonly used method of work measurement for Direct Production Workers is that based on stop-watch measurement of elements. PMTS and SMRA are also sometimes used, and are becoming more popular.

For skilled service workers, the stop-watch is increasingly becoming acceptable. Generally, a combination of stop-watch values, analytical estimating and bench-marks is used.

For staff workers, the stop-watch is sometimes used but it is more usual to adopt a less formal approach to work measurement, using approximate cycle times and dispensing with rating. As it is unusual for pay to be directly related to work done, there is less need for accuracy and more scope for 'taking the rough with the smooth'. Activity sampling is also used in assessing the staffing of offices and other indirect work.

PRODUCTIVITY MEASUREMENT—MEASUREMENT OF CO-OPERATION—LARGE GROUP EFFORT AND EFFECTIVENESS

A measurement of the effective use of labour in large groups, such as departments, can be obtained by productivity measurement.

By productivity is usually meant labour productivity and this can be defined as the ratio of output to the labour hours required to produce that output. If output and labour clock hours—say, for a particular department for a number of consecutive weeks—are plotted on a graph, the result is normally as shown in Fig. 5. The points, representing output and hours for each week, are scattered, but a mean line can often be drawn through the points. Typically, this does not pass through the origin but cuts the 'hours' axis. This is because there is normally a fixed element in the labour hours.

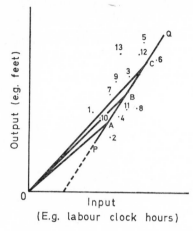

Slopes OA, OB, OC,
measure productivity

Points 1,2,3.....13 etc.
represent 13 consecutive
periods in time

Fig. 5

OUTPUT PLOTTED AGAINST INPUT

In this situation, productivity is the slope of the line from the origin to some point on the relation PQ, i.e. productivity is the gradient of the lines OA, OB, OC, etc. These slopes depend on the level of input and output so that the slope only has meaning at a particular output. This fits with the common-sense idea that productivity will increase naturally as a factory gets busier.

The relationship between output and labour input is affected by a number of factors including:

  i. labour rate of working and effectiveness, both as individuals and as a team;

 ii. changes in activity, i.e. how much of the department's capacity is being utilized;

iii. the mix of work constituting the output;

 iv. changes in work-in-progress;

  v. capital investment;

 vi. management effectiveness.

For discussion with workers' representatives it is necessary to be clear whether the measures of productivity being used are affected by all the above factors. (There may also be additional factors to those listed.) Alternatively, the effect of some of these factors may be eliminated, if it is possible to assess their effect on productivity.

LABOUR PRODUCTIVITY—ALL FACTORS

To establish measures of labour productivity which respond to all the factors affecting it in a department, it is considered that physical measures of output should be used as far as possible. These may be in terms of number, length, area, volume, weight, etc.

Difficulties arise where there are no obvious physical measures, as occurs, for example, in a jobbing machine shop. Sometimes the output can be divided into a number of categories and weighting factors established between one category and another. Sometimes it is necessary to use information provided by estimates. The problems are technical but generally some means can be devised, even if it is finally necessary to use sales value or added value as a measure of output.

The choices relating to the measure of labour input are concerned with:

    i. defining the labour to be included;

    ii. the use of time, clock-hours, days, or weeks, etc., or money;

    iii. the inclusion or exclusion of the effect of overtime.

The effect of activity (i.e. how busy the department is) will be reduced (but not eliminated) if direct labour hours only are used for input. This is because the direct labour hours increase and decrease in line with activity, whereas indirect and service hours do not do so to the same extent. However, the exclusion of indirect hours reduces the comprehensiveness of a productivity index and it is generally preferable to include them.

The disadvantage of using money as an input measure is that its real value changes with time so that to be meaningful, money measures should be corrected to some constant money value basis. For the measurement of labour productivity, clock-hours are a better input measure, and they can be related to money by the cost of labour per clock-hour.

Overtime affects both the cost and the productivity of labour but it is desirable that the effect of overtime on productivity and the effect of the overtime premium on labour cost per hour are separately assessed. For productivity assessment it is therefore recommended that overtime clock-hours are included in the input.

LABOUR PRODUCTIVITY—LABOUR RESPONSIBILITY

It is possible to approach this measure of production from the 'all-factors' measure, by eliminating the effect of all factors except those which are the direct responsibility of labour. This approach has the advantage that the effect of different factors can be separately asssessed and therefore monitored and, perhaps, controlled. It has the disadvantage of requiring a fair degree of statistical technique and also the establishment of procedures to accumulate information, and therefore it takes time. Useful results may be obtained more quickly by the alternative approach of seeking measures of output which start off by intending to measure only the labour contribution to output.

One such measure of output is 'standard minutes' (S.Ms.) produced, where the standard minutes content of output can substantially be obtained from work-measured incentive scheme bookings. Clearly in using such a measure the input hours and the output S.Ms. produced must relate properly. The problems involved concern:

(a) the people and jobs for whom S.Ms. are evaluated, i.e. some people and some jobs may at different times be unmeasured and it is therefore important that the corresponding clock-hours do not appear in the input if the S.M.s do not appear in the output.

(b) the definition of S.Ms. in output. For example, a distinction might be made between directly productive S.M.s (e.g. actual work directly concerned with the output), indirectly productive (e.g. controlled contingencies such as quality checks, cleaning, etc.) and unproductive (e.g. waiting time). If it is intended to make these distinctions, great care must be taken in establishing the definitions and ensuring that they are understood and properly interpreted. It is not necessary to obtain exact correspondence between S.Ms. and actual clock-hours in the categories, directly productive, indirectly productive, and non-productive, to obtain a useful productivity index, but whatever lack of correspondence there is should be borne in mind when interpreting changes in a productivity index based on this approach.

Another output measure is 'estimated labour hours' which is suitable, provided the basis of estimating is sound and is 'frozen' throughout the period of comparison.

Any 'measure of work' derived from any of the work measurement techniques, provides a means of assessing labour controlled output and may be used as long as the considerations discussed above are taken into account.

METHODOLOGY

A productivity ratio, or any other ratio for that matter, should be used with care because quite often it may not provide a suitable basis if the comparison is to be used to understand the effect of various factors and policies.

In the example of Fig. 5 (*see* p. 23) productivity measured by line OB is higher than that measured by line OA. Point B may be a later period than point A and the conclusion might be drawn that greater effort was being put in by the labour force. However, the effect can be completely explained by an increase in volume. It is, therefore, generally safest to plot the outputs and inputs graphically. Well established statistical methods allow the best line to be 'drawn' mathematically, together with an estimate of the accuracy of the line (based on the scatter of the points about the line). Points on the graph can be labelled with a series of consecutive numbers corresponding with the passage of time. The vertical distance of each point from the mean line is measured, above the line being positive, below the line being negative. These vertical distances or offsets can then be replotted on a second graph, which is like a quality control chart (Fig. 6). Each offset is an amount of output by which the actual output exceeds or falls short of the average. This excess or short-fall can be conveniently expressed as a plus or minus percentage of the output and this can be used as a productivity indicator and plotted on the control graph.

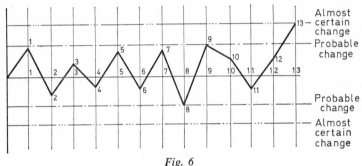

Fig. 6

OFFSETS FROM MEAN OUTPUT/INPUT RELATION PLOTTED CONSECUTIVELY

A by-product of finding the average line statistically is that 'probable' and 'almost certain' lines can be drawn on the control graph (similar to warning and action lines on a quality control graph), which indicate that points falling outside this line (i.e. above or below) probably or almost certainly represent real changes in productivity. Points falling within the 'probable' lines are less likely to indicate real changes in productivity.

If several other factors are expected to affect productivity, then it may be important to separate their effects. Typical factors of this nature are work-in-progress and mix.

Work-in-progress effects may be eliminated by adopting a suitable formula to convert changes in work-in-progress to equivalent output. If this is not done, there is a danger that short-term changes in productivity may be misleading, e.g. a new manager may clear a good deal of work-in-progress from the shop over a period of a month or two, giving rise to an inflated output.

Mix is more difficult to deal with. One approach identifies measurable characteristics of the mix which might be expected to have a substantial effect on the output-input relationship.

Establishing relationships between input and output and the effect of other variables on these relationships may be assisted by categorizing output, i.e. separating one sort of output from another, and hence deriving a number of productivity measures. These separate measures may then be combined as an average, weighted by the content of labour clock-hours.

MEASUREMENT OF THE EFFECT OF RESPONSIBLE SKILL AND THOUGHT IN UTILIZING THE RESOURCES OF THE FIRM

It is virtually impossible to separate the worker's contribution from that of management towards making a firm prosperous. Nevertheless, some means is required to measure prosperity and also to decide how the monetary consequences of prosperity can be shared between workers, the firm, shareholders and the consumer.

An obvious measure of prosperity is profit. Profit sharing has not become popular, however. One drawback of profit sharing is that profits may fluctuate substantially due to causes that are completely outside of the control of the workers.

A measure which has become popular is 'added value'. For a given period of time, this is the total sales income less all items and services purchased outside the firm. One reason why this is a particularly useful concept is due to another principle discovered by Allen W. Rucker. Rucker uses the term 'production value' rather than 'added value'. To quote from 'Harvard Business Review', September–October 1955:

> Labour unions have come to demand an equitable 'share of increasing productivity' as part of their members' earnings.
> . . . Total pay-roll costs of hourly-rated factory labour (direct and indirect, with overtime and premium payment and 'fringes') tend to bear a near-constant relationship to production value. Thus there is a basis for comparing this year's pay-roll with former years' despite changing levels of prices and productivity.
> To give an example:

	£	£
Sales value of output	=150,000	
Deduct all bought out materials, supplies and services	70,000	
Production value		80,000
Labour cost	20,000	
Ratio of labour cost to production value	$=\dfrac{20,000}{80,000}=0.25$	

This is the 'Rucker ratio'.

c

After a firm has established the Rucker ratio the principle can then be adopted of guaranteeing this ratio to the workers in future. If, in the above example, the production value increased to £100,000, then the labour share could be allowed to rise to £25,000. If the extra production was generated without increasing wages cost, then there would be £5,000 to distribute to the workers.

Another approach is to relate a bonus percentage or payment to the Rucker ratio.

RELATIONSHIPS BETWEEN ADDED VALUE AND PRODUCTIVITY

It may be shown that:

$$\frac{\text{Added value (£)}}{\text{Labour cost (£)}} \text{ ,, which is the reverse of the Rucker ratio, is}$$

equal to

$$\frac{\text{Labour productivity (tons/hour)}}{\text{(Cost per hour of labour (£/hour)}} \left[\begin{array}{c} \text{Selling} \\ \text{price} \\ \text{per} \\ \text{ton} \end{array} - \left(\begin{array}{c} \text{Material} \\ \text{cost} \\ \text{per ton} \\ \hline \text{yield} \end{array} + \begin{array}{c} \text{Consumable} \\ \text{cost} \\ \text{per} \\ \text{ton} \end{array} \right) \right]$$

In this statement the measure of output is 'tons' but any other measure of output could apply. Costs are in consistent units, e.g. £. This relationship shows the factors affecting the Rucker ratio, namely:

Labour productivity (e.g. output/man-hour).

Cost per hour of labour.

Selling price per unit of output.

Material cost per unit of output.

Yield=ratio of finished weight of products to raw material input weight.

Consumable cost per unit of output.

Apart from the selling price and purchase price of materials, all the above factors are partially within the control of the workers. The ratio can be converted to constant selling and material purchasing prices over a period of time, if this is thought desirable.

If the inverse ratio is converted to constant values of selling price per ton, material cost per ton, yield, and consumable cost per ton, then the relation becomes:

$$\frac{\text{Added value (£)}}{\text{Labour cost (£)}} = \frac{\text{Labour productivity}}{\text{Cost per hour of labour}} \times \text{constant}$$

Thus, added value, adjusted in this way, provides another means of measuring labour productivity.

3

Management's Contribution to Productivity Improvement

In a comprehensive productivity bargain, the important objectives are ultimately concerned with increasing the ratio of added value to labour cost. To recapitulate, added value is the difference between sales income and expenditure on bought out direct production materials, consumables and services. Labour cost depends on the cost per hour of labour and on labour productivity, i.e., output per man hour.

In the previous chapter, the ways in which workers can contribute to increasing productivity and added value have been discussed. Management has an equally vital part to play for it can augment the workers' contributions substantially.

There are available to management a range of techniques which have been proven to be effective in reducing costs and improving efficiency. These techniques include method study, work simplification, value analysis, variety reduction, formal cost reduction programmes; and on the clerical side, O & M. It is usual for these techniques to be introduced and applied by external consultants or by internal specialists. Successful application requires that there is involvement in practical application by both general management and the workers concerned. The techniques themselves are simple and in principle there is no reason why anyone should not use them. In practice, they rely on considerable human relation skills because there is usually much resistance to the innovations that are involved. Sound administrative procedures and availablity of trained staff to follow up the inevitable numerous details are required. Although workers can contribute significantly to this work and should be given every encouragement to do so, it is management which must give the lead.

Independently and by co-operating together, management and workers will produce improvements in such directions as increasing output rates, reducing manning, saving scrap and consumables and so on. It is essential for management to realize that these benefits are initially only opportunities. Executive management have to translate them into real benefits measured in trading statement terms. For example, reducing labour in one area is of little value if it is merely transferred to another area where it is surplus to requirements. Increasing output rates must not be squandered by increases in waiting time. Management thus has a further responsibility beyond directly increasing productivity and added value. This is to be discharged in the exercise of good management throughout the firm by, for example, the installation and operation of sound control systems (quality control, production control, maintenance control, cost control, etc.) and effective corporate planning, marketing and capital investment.

The purpose of this chapter is not to pursue the subject of effective management, although it is a legitimate interest to all concerned in a productivity bargain. Rather it is to describe some of the useful efficiency improvement techniques which are primarily management's responsibility but to which the workers can often make valuable contributions. These will be considered in relation to:

    i.   improving labour productivity.
   ii.   improving value.
  iii.   reducing direct production material and consumable costs.
  iv.   formalized cost reductions.

The techniques described have found widest application in production work but they can be used anywhere—in maintenance, building work, clerical work, laboratories, drawing offices and in any industry or activity. When they are applied to a particular area, they are often given a label. Thus O & M (organization and methods) is often a loosely used synonym for method study in the office.

IMPROVING LABOUR PRODUCTIVITY

The techniques involved here are all variants of method study which is defined as 'The systematic recording and critical examination of existing and proposed ways of doing work as a means of developing and applying easier and more effective methods and reducing costs.'

This indicates the basic techniques of the various systems of method study which are:

(a) techniques of obtaining information—ranging from asking questions and visual observation to the use of cine films or tape recorders, etc.

(b) techniques of displaying and presenting information—usually the heart of the technique involving a wide variety of charts showing the interactions of men and machines both in time and in two or three dimensions, i.e. in plan or spatially.

(c) techniques of review, appraisal and examination which normally involve a point of view, i.e. eliminating processes, reducing inspections, transports, storages and delays, reducing variety.

(d) improving methods—where the new methods are evolved from the existing methods.

As examples, five techniques are briefly described:

QUESTIONS AND CHECK LISTS

To someone experienced in a particular industry, a great deal of benefit can be obtained from using a formalized questioning technique. The most common questions that can be asked are:

1. The purpose of the job—is it necessary? Can it be eliminated in whole or in part?
2. The location of the job—is it in the right place?
3. The position of the job in sequences of other jobs—is this right?
4. The person doing the job—is this the best person to do it?
5. The means by which the job is done—is there a better way?

Check lists serve a similar purpose. Many of these appear from time to time in some of the publications listed in the Bibliography.

PROCESS ELIMINATION

This is a simple approach which seeks to eliminate a process or operation altogether. Each operation is examined very carefully to see if it can be eliminated. This is generally simpler than it sounds, for many industrial operations consist of a series of operations, some of which are duplicated. For example, it is not unusual for items to be counted on completion in one department and again on receipt in another department. Duplication is particularly rife in clerical operations but can generally be found everywhere. Apart from duplication, a great many operations are self-cancelling. Then there are the operations carried out to put something right that should never have gone wrong. Industrial life is full of operations such as correcting, fettling, cleaning up, filing off, straightening, flattening, smoothing, etc. Sometimes operations can be eliminated by merging them with others or getting several things done at the same time.

WORK SIMPLIFICATION

Work simplification depends on identifying the five activities of: operations, inspections, transports, storages and delays, and recognizing that of these, only operations really add any value (and it is possible that some of these are unnecessary as well). The object in work simplification then is to eliminate or reduce inspections, transports, storages and delays.

A study of all the inspections taking place in a process can generally lead to an elimination of some of them, as there is frequently much duplication. Sometimes the cost of an inspection is greater than the errors it seeks to eliminate. The use of Statistical Quality Control frequently allows an adequate amount of inspection to be obtained at a reduced cost by sampling only a proportion of the total to be inspected.

Transports can often be eliminated, for example, by careful study of routing to avoid back tracking. If the transports cannot be eliminated, they can generally be reduced; again by better layout or the use of various items of mechanical handling and storage equipment.

Storages can be avoided—or rather the cost of putting an item into or drawing it out of a store—by so organizing the flow of work that it becomes unnecessary. This has been well done by the car manufacturers who hold very small stores. The storage is really taking place in the pipeline of supplies, i.e. the lorries and dispatch areas of suppliers. Conveyors are another form of pipeline to avoid storage. And if a storage cannot be eliminated, then it can generally be reduced.

Delays, if knowingly planned into the process, have to be attacked at source, i.e. the reasons for planning the delay have to be examined. The delay may be, for example, to allow something to cool down or heat up; and it may be possible to eliminate or reduce it. Unplanned delays clearly should not occur. Careful provision should be made to see that all delays are recorded and analysed by cause, so that the causes can be eradicated.

IMPROVING VALUE

To be in profitable business it is necessary when making a product, to ensure that the value to the customer is greater than the cost to the manufacturer.

Customers can be interested in two types of value:
1. the value of the usefulness and/or performance of the product.
2. the value, independent of the product's usefulness or performance, that makes him want to buy and own it.

Every attribute, piece and part of an object should contribute use and/or performance, and/or should cause customers to want to buy it.

The object of value analysis is to investigate the relationship between costs and value to the customer in order to be able to achieve a given value at minimum cost or maximum value for a given cost.

In practice, the technique consists of taking a manufactured object, analysing it into its various parts and then for each part, listing the functions and the various features of the part. Next the costs for each part and each feature are carefully analysed, process-by-process. Like so many of the efficiency techniques, value analysis depends on an infinite capacity for taking pains and much of the searching and sifting of detail throws up, for anyone who is on the look-out, clear cut opportunities to avoid waste of money.

In the phases of obtaining, recording and presenting information, value analysis has much in common with method study, but there is a predominant emphasis on detailed costs and the value of each process and product feature.

The review phase of value analysis is the creative part and involves a small group of people with knowledge of customers, costs, materials, methods and process, who examine the facts presented to them and seek to identify the essential functions and features and the cheapest way to provide these, having regard to the intangible values which an object possesses independent of its usefulness or performance. Value analysis can also be applied advantageously at the design stage of a product.

In practice, this apparently simple, common-sense approach rarely fails to save less than 10 per cent of the cost of any object to which it is applied.

VARIETY REDUCTION

Variety reduction is a rather more expressive name for the well-known idea of standardization. Variety may be the spice of life, but it is no help at all to efficiency. This is because variety is the opponent of volume, i.e. the more variety there is, the less the quantity of each set, each model, each type. Henry Ford was quick to see that variety reduction was the key to reducing cost in the motor industry with his dictum, 'You can have any colour you like, so long as it's black.' Too much variety has been thought by many to be one of the causes for low productivity in Britain—the home of the custom-built tailor-made article. Variety reduction is the first step towards large quantity production, mechanization and automation.

In making and selling goods for sale, there is always a pressure from the sales people to produce yet another variety or line, which is just what the market is waiting for. From time to time, therefore, new varieties are added but rarely are any of the old ones discarded, so that before long, the manufacturing people are making dozens, hundreds or even thousands of different articles with small runs. It is not uncommon to find factories where the possible number of variants are measured in hundreds of thousands, or even millions.

The technique of variety reduction is simply to seek ways and means of reducing variety. One of the ways is to identify those variants which are infrequently sold, asked for, used, etc. and to eliminate them.

It is generally only necessary to collect the information, say, on the variety of products or forms or electric motors or typewriters used —for the opportunity for variety reduction to be disclosed. The main problem is to achieve agreement amongst all those involved as to which variants should be eliminated.

REDUCING DIRECT PRODUCTION MATERIAL AND CONSUMABLE COSTS

The unit cost of purchasing direct materials can often be reduced by value analysis allied to efficient and knowledgeable purchasing.

Some examples are:

    i. Efficient purchasing, by continuous comparison of prices and continuous pressure on suppliers to reduce prices. With some companies, this goes to the extent of offering suppliers assistance in applying efficiency techniques to themselves.

    ii. Seeking and obtaining quantity discounts.

    iii. Purchasing in bulk and/or in semi-finished condition.

    iv. Applying value analysis to clarify the exact function of purchases so that cheaper alternatives can be sought.

    v. Reducing as far as possible the variety of purchases.

    vi. Obtaining the best possible price for scrap.

The reduction of the amount of direct materials used per unit of output is often a very substantial source of cost reduction. Some ways in which this can be done are:

    i. Reducing the number of defective products which are either rejected during manufacture (including the final inspection stages) or are subsequently returned from customers.

    ii. Reducing the amount of product which is made excess to customer's requirements. This can occur through error or through lack of process or quality control in certain industries.

    iii. Reducing the amount of direct material that is lost as a result of manufacture, e.g. evaporation, scaling, machine chips and turnings, cuttings, etc. Frequently as much as 50 per cent of direct materials are lost in this way.

    iv. Applying incentives designed to motivate people to make the best possible use of direct production materials. This involves devising methods of measuring the usage of direct production materials, in relation to output.

    v. Using value analysis to reduce the amount of direct production material per unit of output.

The use of consumables per unit of output can be reduced by:

    i. establishing careful control over consumable usage, e.g. measurement of usage and control over authorization to obtain items from stores,

    ii. making everyone aware of the cost of consumables by various means, e.g. notice-boards, posters, displays of frequently used consumables with prices, etc.,

    iii. studying methods of reducing the use of consumables by using method study principles devoted to this end. This involves considering each major consumable in turn and examining the factors affecting its use and available methods of reducing consumption,

    iv. salvaging, or re-using consumables,

    v. applying incentives designed to reduce consumable usage.

FORMALIZED COST REDUCTION

A cost reduction is defined as a reduction in the cost of making something or carrying out some operation resulting from conscious, planned action.

Generally, cost reductions are restricted to reductions in *direct* costs, that is wages, materials used in the product, and consumables such as fuel, heat, electricity, tools, etc., used to make the product. A cost reduction is therefore generally one of the four things that the techniques already described have been designed to improve:

i.   an increase in the *rate* of production, i.e. more items, operations, etc. per hour.

ii. a reduction in wage cost per hour, such as could result from a reduction in a team to carry out a job, say, from four men to three men.

iii. a reduction in the amount of direct material lost as scrap in one way or another. (By direct material, is meant the material(s) of which the item is made.)

iv. a reduction in the amount of consumables used per item or per hour.

There are a number of problems which arise in the application of the various efficiency improvement techniques which formalized cost reduction is designed to overcome. These are:

i.   resistance to change—which is often manifest by a reluctance to implement new ideas.

ii. difficulties of progressing and obtaining progress on the multitude of actions necessary to bring new ideas to the stage of practical application.

iii. assessing the value of cost reductions in a way that is universally credible.

The starting point for formalized cost reduction is the acceptance of the principle that those who are responsible for spending money must be the ones who are responsible for cost reduction.

In a company, this is usually the departmental head. If he has a department of some 250 people, he may be responsible for spending money to the extent of £½–£1 million on wages, salaries, materials, machines, maintenance, and so on. Many foremen are responsible for spending £100,000 a year, or more.

To achieve substantial cost reductions, what is required therefore is a team of from six to twelve people, led by the departmental head and containing his immediate subordinates, and any others who are interested and able to help. This ensures involvement of all concerned. It is important to include anyone in the team who might otherwise resist change.

FORMING THE COST REDUCTION TEAM

The Departmental Manager, as soon as he is convinced and enthusiastic, nominates his team, informs the members, and arranges their first meeting. At the meeting it is useful to have some independent person to talk about costs and productivity, prices and incomes and to establish the vital importance of reducing costs. Each member is then asked to think about ways and ideas of saving money and increasing efficiency, and to be ready to table them at the next meeting of the team. The point is made at this stage that cost reduction does not mean not spending money. On the contrary it may mean spending more money to reduce the cost per unit of output. It is not being penny wise and pound foolish. It is getting better value for money.

At the second meeting, various proposals are discussed and those that are considered promising by all concerned are listed. By the conclusion of the meeting, a number of ideas will have been put forward and the next job is to assess the cost of the schemes, and the likely savings. Whenever possible this should be done by or with the active assistance and collaboration of the company accountants.

At the third meeting, the team considers again the various proposals and examines the costs and savings. After discussion, the schemes which seem likely to produce good savings are authorized to proceed. Further items may be raised.

Before long, it is possible to produce a list or programme of cost reduction items and it is frequently surprising and gratifying for the members of the team to see what the forecast savings of the programme add up to—it is generally of the order of thousands of pounds.

An important task in administering a cost reduction programme is the detailed progressing of the many steps involved in each of a large number of cost reduction projects.

The work of progressing is best carried out by a method study engineer, for he can also be developing ideas and projects to bring before the cost reduction team. Most of the implementation will actually be done by engineers and production people, but other service functions may be involved. The method study engineer can also, with advantage, be made the secretary of the cost deduction team.

REPORTING AND ACCOUNTING

As a Cost Reduction Scheme approaches the day of implementation, calculations should be made—with better information now than when the idea was first proposed—on the expected savings. This checks that it is still worthwhile to implement. The accountants, who should check all forecasts of savings, can also see these calculations which give them some idea of the form which the final calculations will take.

When the item is implemented and has been operating satisfactorily for some weeks, a final set of calculations is produced based on the actual results obtained. This set of calculations is then vetted by the accountants and agreed or amended as necessary.

CATEGORY OF COST	DEPT A	DEPT B			TOTAL		
Direct Materials							
Direct Productive Labour							
Consumables							
TOTAL PRIMARY COSTS							
Indirect Labour							
Maintenance and Service Labour							
Works Admin. Salaries							
Maintenance Materials							
Depreciation							
Miscellaneous Works Expenses							
Mis. Works Admin. Expenses							
TOTAL SECONDARY COSTS							
General Admin.							
Selling							
Distribution							
Buildings							
GENERAL COSTS							
TOTAL COSTS							

Fig. 7

EXAMPLE OF A FORM OF ANALYSIS OF COSTS

Once a month, or quarterly, the implemented schemes are listed and totalled to provide a value of cost reductions implemented in the month or quarter. This statement should then be signed by a Senior Accountant as representing an agreed Company statement of savings.

The simplest and most useful way to present savings is in terms of the amount of money that each project will save in a year, i.e. savings are stated at an annual rate.

EVALUATING THE POTENTIAL COST REDUCTION

As part of the work of assessing the financial case for a productivity bargain, it is helpful to be able to assess the overall potential for cost reduction in a company. This also provides strong motivation to obtain the cost reductions and a basis for setting targets.

The starting point for this work is a categorization of costs. For example, this might be into:

Primary costs	Direct materials.
	Direct productive labour.
	Consumables.
Secondary costs	Indirect labour.
	Maintenance and service labour.
	Works administration, wages and salaries.
	Maintenance materials.
	Depreciation.
	Miscellaneous works expenses.
	Miscellaneous works administration expenses.
General costs	General Administration.
	Selling.
	Distribution.
	Buildings.

These costs are also categorized by Departments and a typical analysis form is illustrated in Fig. 7. This enables it to be seen which are the important costs and which are relatively unimportant.

Next, for each category of costs in each Department, an estimate is made of the potential percentage reduction. This potential should be realistic but it should not take too much account of ways and means. It is meant to represent the difference between the present costs and the absolute rock bottom costs that could be achieved if everything were done and every effort were made by all concerned, i.e. workers and management. An example is shown in the Table of Fig. 8 where the first column repeats the analysis of costs, the second column shows each cost as a percentage of the total cost and the third column shows the potential for cost reduction for each cost. In the fourth and fifth columns the percentage potential for cost reduction is multiplied by the costs and percentage costs, to give the potential cost reduction as a money value and as a percentage of total costs. This analysis provides

EXAMPLE OF FORM OF ANALYSIS OF POTENTIAL FOR COST REDUCTION

Department..................

CATEGORY OF COST	COST £	% OF TOTAL COSTS	MAX. POTENTIAL FOR COST REDUCTION %	MAX. POTENTIAL FOR COST REDUCTION £	MAX. POTENTIAL FOR COST REDUCTION AS A PERCENTAGE OF TOTAL COSTS
Direct Materials	410	58.3	5	20.5	2.92
Direct Productive Labour	90	12.8	25	22.5	3.2
Consumables	36	5.1	10	3.6	.51
TOTAL PRIMARY COST	536	76.2		46.6	6.63
Indirect Labour	10	1.4	25	2.5	.35
Maintenance and Service Labour	25	3.6	25	6.25	.90
Works Admin. Salaries	40	5.7	25	10.0	1.43
Maintenance Materials	30	4.3	5	1.5	.21
Depreciation	10	1.4	—	—	—
Miscellaneous Works Expenses	2	.3	10	.2	.03
Mis. Works Admin. Expenses	7	1.0	20	1.4	.2
TOTAL SECONDARY COSTS	124	17.7		21.85	3.12
General Admin.	2	.3	20	.4	.06
Selling	2	.3	20	.4	.06
Distribution	12	1.7	5	.6	.09
Buildings	24	3.4	5	1.2	.17
GENERAL COSTS	40	6.1		2.6	.38
TOTAL COSTS	700	100		71.05	10.13

Fig. 8 EXAMPLE OF A FORM OF ANALYSIS OF POTENTIAL FOR COST REDUCTION

a clearer picture of where savings can be obtained and consequently where the effort should be concentrated.

A second analysis that should be carried out is to analyse all costs into responsibility areas so that each foreman, manager, executive and director is quite clear about the amount of money he is responsible for spending. Ideally, this should again be split into the various expense categories, in so far as these are appropriate. If this is done, then each member of management should estimate the potential for cost reductions, taking what advice he may require, so that a complete picture is built of costs, who is responsible for them and what potential there is to reduce them. As the management tree is ascended, so the costs accumulate at each level—thus a manager may be responsible for the costs incurred by say his five foremen plus some additional ones which are his own responsibility.

Thirdly, the same sort of analysis should be done for each cost reduction team—frequently this will be the same as the Departmental Managers' analyses.

The analyses also provide the framework for monitoring results, for as each cost reduction is obtained it can be slotted into its appropriate niche and from time to time progress towards the ultimate targets can be assessed.

EXTENT OF WORKER PARTICIPATION

The topics discussed in this chapter are essentially concerned with management, but every opportunity should be taken of involving the work people concerned.

A traditional and useful means of involvement is through suggestion schemes, where suggestions are individually rewarded. However, where workers are obtaining some benefits from increasing productivity and/or added value, they can more readily be brought into what has hitherto been regarded as the management activities of efficiency improvement.

Formalized cost reduction provides a useful way of involving workers by having them elect representatives to the departmental cost reduction teams. Work simplification can also be taught quickly to all workers, who can then be encouraged to study their own work and to report their findings to the cost reduction team.

4

Job Evaluation and Wages Structure

JOB EVALUATION

It is impossible to build a satisfactory wages structure unless the fundamental values of the jobs in relation to one another are right and are accepted as right. In some companies, especially very small ones, the right relationship of jobs might have been arrived at by trial and error or rule of thumb. Most companies need to use something more methodized to establish the relative worth of jobs, and one or other of the methods of job evaluation described below will fit the bill in most cases. The descriptions given convey the fundamental characteristics of each system. There are many variations on these basic themes and many refinements which can be made to suit particular applications. In all of the systems and all of the applications it is important that everybody understands that job evaluation is concerned only with the basic job and not with the above or below average performances which Tom, Dick or Harry bring to the job as individuals.

THE JOB DESCRIPTION

It is obviously unreasonable to attempt comparisons between jobs without some basic data. This is provided by the Job Description and may be supplemented by observation of the job and questioning the incumbent and other knowledgeable people. The job description may be either brief and simple or detailed, and the choice will depend largely on the type of evaluation method which is to be used. Even the most detailed job descriptions should however be as brief and simple as possible. As with so many techniques, it is very easy in job evaluation to introduce such a wealth of detail and parapharnalia that the technique becomes an end in itself instead of the means to an end. A typical job description will take the following pattern. It can be reduced or extended in detail as the method of evaluation demands

Job Title :	Painter and Decorator
Department :	Maintenance
Summary :	Interior and exterior decoration of factory and office buildings and glazing.

Content

Prepares surfaces prior to decorating by stripping, washing or rubbing down, applying putty or other fillers, followed by priming or sizing depending on finish. Applies paint by brush, roller or spray-gun. Undertakes glazing repairs, measuring and cutting suitable glass. Maintains paintwork by washing down at prescribed intervals, using detergents or degreasers. Erects scaffolding with assistance and under supervision. Keeps painters' shop tidy and disposes of waste glass, wallpaper, etc.

Job Requirements

Apprenticeship or similar basic training. Comprehensive knowledge of primers and paints and ceiling and wall coverings for varying conditions (wet, greasy, hot). High degree of hand and eye co-ordination.

Responsibility and Mental Requirements

Plans and carries out work with minimum of guidance and supervision. Occasional control of one or two labourers. No responsibility for expensive equipment but responsible for safe working practices and maintaining ladders, scaffolding, trestles, etc. in a safe condition.

Physical Requirements and Conditions

Fairly high physical effort, working on ladders, scaffolding and roofs. Carries material (including glass) to location, necessitating use of ladders, etc. for high work. Regular contact with paint, chemical paint solvents. Much of work is outside, though not usually in highly inclement conditions.

The most important ingredient for successful job evaluation is the acceptability of the results to the employees concerned. Managements can carry out job evaluation without any participation by the employees side, but the results will rarely be as acceptable as when there is full involvement of both parties. It is recommended that this full involvement starts with joint consideration of the various methods which might be used. A short introductory course, conducted by experienced people, and attended by the appropriate representatives of management and employees, is a particularly valuable way of triggering off positive involvement. Such a course, which should preferably take place on the company's premises, should include short joint exercises on methods of evaluation such as the following:

RANKING

From short job descriptions, jobs are placed in order of importance or relative value. The ranking order for a toolmaker, a labourer, a painter and a machine greaser would probably be

1. Toolmaker   3. Machine greaser
2. Painter   4. Labourer

Ranking is easy and quick to instal if there are not very many jobs to be considered. It is something of a blunt instrument, however, and it quickly becomes unwieldy as the number of jobs to be dealt with increases.

GRADING (OR CLASSIFICATION)

Another disadvantage of ranking is that it gives no indication of where the grade lines should be drawn between groups of jobs. The grading system starts off by defining the grades and the task of the evaluators is then to slot jobs into the appropriate grades. Grades might be defined as follows:

Grade A: No previous experience needed. Each task is allotted and closely supervised. Working conditions not exceptional but there may be an amount of physical effort.

Grade B: Routine and repetitive work but a comparatively short period of training or experience is needed. Some heavy lifting, unpleasant conditions or exceptional physical effort may be involved. Close supervision but expected to observe and correct minor quality variations in his work.

The final grade might be:

Grade G: Apprenticeship or similar comprehensive training. Detailed knowledge of tools of trade. Works to fine limits and uses considerable measure of discretion and initiative with the minimum of supervision.

In such a grading the labourer would probably be put in Grade A, the machine greaser in Grade B, and the toolmaker in Grade G.

Grading, like Ranking, is somewhat arbitrary and is more likely to be successful where there are relatively few jobs involved.

FACTOR COMPARISON

Ranking and Grading are quick, easy and imprecise. Factor Comparison slowly and laboriously searches for precision.

The aim is to identify the main factors present in the jobs in a company and then to rank or allot values for each job under each factor heading.

Skill	Responsibility	Effort	Working Conditions
Toolmaker	Toolmaker	Labourer	Greaser
Painter	Painter	Greaser	Labourer
Greaser	Greaser	Painter	Painter
Labourer	Labourer	Toolmaker	Toolmaker

The factor headings are usually weighted so that 'skill' for instance, would yield more value than 'effort' for the same rank. An overall rank order based on the various factor rankings can then be prepared.

D

As a refinement the evaluators can decide how much of each job's current wage rate should be allotted under each factor. For example, if half the toolmaker's rate is considered to derive from his skill, then half his hourly rate will be entered against him in the 'skill' column. When this has been done for all the factors of all the jobs, the two exercises—the factor ranking and the money value allocation—can be compared for consistency. There is usually a good deal of reconciliation and adjustment. Even without the 'money value' refinement, factor comparison is a lengthy process, and it is significant that, of the companies who use job evaluation, only about 5 per cent use the factor comparison method.

POINTS RATING

In terms of popularity, points rating is at the other end of the scale to factor comparison. This is because the principle is easy to understand and because it appears to be a reasonably detached and precise method. Factors similar to those in factor comparison are used and the evaluators agree on the number of points each job scores under each factor. The maximum points allowed vary from factor to factor, depending on the relative importance of each factor within the company setting. An example is:

Job	Skill (max. 35)	Responsi- bility (max. 30)	Effort (max. 20)	Working Cond'n. (max. 15)	Total (max. 100)
Toolmaker	35	26	5	3	69
Painter	27	18	10	7	62
Greaser	3	6	16	15	40
Labourer	0	2	20	11	33

The major disadvantage of the points system is that it is usually a long-winded process, though not to the same extent as factor comparison.

PAIRED COMPARISONS (DIRECT CONSENSUS)

The philosophy of paired comparisons is that attempts at pseudo-scientific measurement should be thrown out of the window and replaced by the acceptance that people in a factory or office inevitably form ideas of the relative value of jobs. A consensus of these ideas of the relative job values will therefore provide the most widely acceptable evaluation of jobs. It is not practicable to involve everyone in the paired comparisons evaluation but very many more people can participate than in the other methods of evaluation.

The evaluators are given forms compiled in such a way that each job is compared in turn with each other job. An evaluator simply has to say which he thinks is the more important or whether they are equal. A paired comparisons form, ready for the judge's ticks, might look like this.

LH Job Title	LH job higher	Both same	RH job higher	RH Job Title
Toolmaker				Painter
Toolmaker				Labourer
Toolmaker				Greaser
Toolmaker				Electrician
Painter				Labourer
Painter				Greaser
Painter				Electrician
Labourer				Greaser
Labourer				Electrician
Greaser				Electrician

It will be seen from this example that it does not take very many jobs to produce a large number of comparisons. Ten judges each comparing forty jobs would produce 7,800 comparisons. The comparisons are however, very quickly done and computer assistance is readily available to process the results and produce the consensus ranking of jobs. Paired comparisons is a much more speedy and reliable method of ranking than the manual method described. Inconsistencies of a judge's comparisons, or inconsistencies betwen judges are quickly revealed. Paired comparisons can be further refined to produce a ranking under job factors, but this will rarely be necessary.

ANALYTICAL TECHNIQUES APPLIED TO POINTS SYSTEMS,
FACTOR COMPARISON AND GRADING

The time taken for these methods can be much reduced by the use of appropriate analytical techniques. Where, for instance, a points system uses a number of factors the statistical mathematical technique of Multiple Regression Analysis may be used to establish the average weights applicable to each factor. Regression Analysis is also valuable in factor comparison if it is decided to establish the amount of current wage attributable to each factor. Grading or classification can more quickly be carried out individually and statistical analysis used to ascertain which jobs are borderline or 'rogue'.

These and similar techniques of mathematical statistics may be obtained in computer 'packages'. They should be applied with caution, but their use will often reduce the time for these methods of job evaluation by a half or more.

WAGES STRUCTURE

A number of elements make up the wage of a worker. The basic wage is often a nationally negotiated wage rate which is either a minimum rate or a standard rate. In the past, this national rate was substantially similar to that actually being paid in each individual factory. Today, however, there are a number of additions: reductions in the number of hours constituting the normal week have given rise to more time being paid at overtime rates; the move towards shift working has meant that shift premiums now represent an important element of wages; there is frequently the addition of payment-by-results bonus.

A typical wage may therefore be made up as follows:

Base rate
Overtime
Shift premium
Bonus.

This structure is designed to achieve:

(a) the attraction of workers to the factory by ensuring that the total earnings are sufficient for this purpose;
(b) willingness of workers to do overtime;
(c) willingness of workers to work shifts;
(d) a high rate of working through incentive bonus or in more general terms, a high rate of contribution from the worker towards achieving the objectives of the factory.

There may be various other allowances in order to obtain willingness on the part of workers to work in dirty, hot or wet conditions, or to work away from home or at height, etc.

The wage structure should be designed to achieve the best compromise between the needs of the company and those of the work people.

THE BASE RATE

This is sometimes called a basic rate or a 'fall-back' rate. It is the minimum a worker can get for doing, or waiting to do, his job. It is usually more than the nationally agreed minimum rate, and may or may not be used for the calculation of overtime, holiday, shift and similar payments. The base rate structure is the cornerstone of the wages structure and it should be built on a sound foundation of job evaluation.

In many companies, years of negotiating on wage rates job by job have resulted in a large number of rates being paid, often with very small differences from one job to the next. When the worth of jobs has been assessed by job evaluation, jobs can be grouped into a small number of payment grades—usually between three and twelve. This greatly simplifies the wages structure and makes it easier to understand and administer. Such a simplification is generally one objective of a productivity bargain.

OVERTIME PAYMENTS

Overtime payments are usually the subject of industry-wide agreements, but they are often varied, or added to, in accordance with the difficulty of motivating people to work extra hours. There has been a tendency in some industries for substantial overtime to be regarded as a permanent feature of the wages structure. Excessive overtime is usually undesirable for it generally is accompanied by low productivity and absenteeism. Reduction of overtime is frequently an objective of a productivity bargain and is achieved by providing better earnings opportunities during the normal working hours or by the rearrangement of working hours, e.g. by shifts.

SHIFT PAYMENTS

Shift payments also have to reflect and overcome the reluctance of workers to work shifts. There are a number of shift patterns in general use including:

 double day shift,
 permanent day and permanent night shift,
 alternating day and night shift,
 three-shift working,
 four-shift working covering a full calendar week.

The amount of premium that it is necessary to pay will vary with the type of shift system, whether the shift is worked during the day or at night and also with the social conditions and alternative employment in the district from which the firm draws its workers. Shift working is usually costly and it is as well to compare the total costs (including the cost of extra supervision) with the benefits expected before deciding it would be advantageous.

BONUS SCHEMES

An adequate structure of base rates, overtime and shift premiums merely ensures the attendance of the worker. By linking pay and performance, incentive bonus schemes represent an attempt to ensure that payments are made only when there are balancing benefits to the company. This is in the spirit of a productivity bargain. Unfortunately, if incentive schemes are to provide a strong motivation, they do tend to disrupt a job evaluated wages structure. This is because it is difficult to provide equal opportunities for earning incentive bonus throughout a firm and over a period of years.

Bonus schemes are subject to a great deal of pressure by workers and management and there is good evidence that they are responsible for some inflationary drift. The view is held strongly in many quarters that incentives (or payment-by-results) are harmful, not only in accelerating wages drift, but in disrupting labour relations.

Even so, the practical experience is that in many factories higher productivity is obtained by using monetary incentives and it is likely that they will continue to be widely used. Where they are used it is to be hoped that managements will appreciate the importance of regularly checking them, and will be mindful of the additional labour relations care.

The link between pay and productivity is an inherent feature of a productivity bargain and the various ways in which this link may be established is now described in some detail. Where incentive schemes have been in existence in a firm for a number of years, it is likely that they will have undergone modifications and that a large number of variants will have resulted. This will have made the wages structure even more difficult to understand and control. Part of the work of introducing a productivity bargain in this situation will be to rationalize the incentive schemes to a uniform pattern and to remove all anomalies in earnings opportunities.

STABILITY OF EARNINGS

More and more workers have regular weekly commitments to meet and a frequently occurring requirement in productivity bargaining is for greater stability of earnings.

Variations of earnings between one week and another generally arise from variations in bonus payments. There may be other causes —differing amounts of overtime will also have the same effect.

There are several causes of bonus payments changing week by week.

  i. For the same effort, it may be possible to earn more bonus on some jobs than on others. The bonus earned in a week would therefore vary according to which jobs a man may do.

 ii. Shortcomings in quality and production control may give rise to varying amounts of waiting time, which may be paid at a lower rate.

iii. Small variations in the variables affecting a process may cause large variations in work content and this may not be taken into account in the assessment of the standard time to do the job.

The requirement to stabilize earnings can be met by eliminating bonus payment altogether. Measured day-work enables this to be done without eliminating the motivation to work.

A shallow incentive will be subject to less variation than a steep one but would be expected to motivate less powerfully. However, stability can be obtained without reducing the strength of the incentive by several means.

  i. By extending the period of time over which performance is measured, e.g. performance may be measured over a period of four weeks rather than one week. This will have the effect of reducing variations in performance by half. Bonus payment may be paid at the four weeks' average rate over the succeeding four weeks. Alternatively, performance may be measured as a moving average, e.g. a four-weekly moving average. Bonus payment will vary from week to week but again the variation should be about half of the straight week-by-week variation.

ii. By using a small number of steps instead of a continuous line in the relation between performance and bonus. Thus a range of performances within a step or band will earn the same bonus. Some overlap of these bonus bands will further assist in stabilizing payment.

iii. By having a fairly limited range of bonus payment. Bonus earned in excess of the maximum is banked and used to supplement the bonus when it falls below the minimum level.

MOTIVATIONAL SYSTEMS

The methods of measuring workers' contributions have already been discussed in Chapter 2. The motivational systems considered here concern the way in which monetary reward is related to these contributions. It will be recollected that three types of contribution were identified together with appropriate methods of measurement as follows:

i. Individual and small group effort and effectiveness—work measurement.

ii Large group effort and effectiveness—productivity measurement.

iii. Measurement of the effect of responsible skill and thought in utilizing the resources of the firm—value added measures.

INDIVIDUAL AND SMALL GROUP SCHEMES
RELATION BETWEEN EARNINGS AND PERFORMANCE

In the context of relating earnings and performance, it is usual to define an hourly rate of earnings as a base. This may be different from any nationally negotiated base rate. It may also be different from the rate on which holiday pay, shift allowances and so on are based. Equally, on occasions these rates may coincide. To avoid confusion here, the base rate which is relevant will be called the incentive earnings base rate (IE base rate).

This IE base rate is generally taken to be the hourly rate to be paid in the absence of any monetary performance-related motivation. For the purpose of the graphical illustrations which follow, this IE base rate is given the value 75 per cent.

The performance relative to the IE base rate is equally given the value 75 per cent. This has the advantage that it follows the implications of the British Standard rating scale where 75 performance is a time (i.e. non-incentive) rate of working. To this extent, a 75 performance has some absolute validity, i.e. it is defined in terms of rating films or a stated performance in the carrying out of some highly formalized activity such as dealing a pack of cards. However a 75 performance can also be allocated arbitrarily to a base rate performance—this is frequently done by implication in productivity bonus schemes where the productivity for an historical base period is taken as being equivalent to 75 per cent. A further advantage of this convention is the possibility of operating a bonus scheme combining individual performance and group (departmental) performance in varying proportions—through the use of a common performance scale.

Clearly infinite variety is possible in the relation between earnings (E) and performance (P) and some typical examples follow:

  i. Directly proportional incentive with guaranteed minimum earnings. This provides a strong incentive effect, which is maintained if all wage increases are consolidated in the base rate, as this basis implied. (Fig. 9).

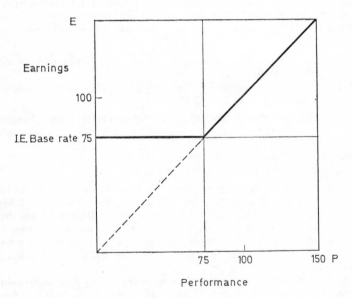

Fig. 9

DIRECTLY PROPORTIONAL INCENTIVE

ii. Less than directly proportional incentive with guaranteed minimum earnings. Variations of this type of scheme have been known as the Halsey Plan, the Bedaux Plan and the Haynes Plan (Fig. 10).

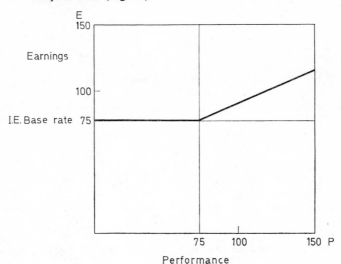

Fig. 10

LESS THAN DIRECTLY PROPORTIONAL INCENTIVE

iii. Directly proportional incentive on only part of the base rate. This provides a weaker incentive effect, which weakens further with time, if wage increases do not affect that part of the base rate to which the directly proportional incentive applies (Fig. 11).

iv. Less than directly proportional incentive starting at less than standard performance (Fig. 12).

v. Accelerating geared scheme—where the increasing difficulty of getting more and more output is recognized and rewarded. This is not often used for fear the scheme will result in excessive bonus payments (Fig. 13).

vi. Decelerating geared scheme—with or without a limit on earnings. This type of scheme is often used where the accuracy of the measurement of performance is in doubt. An example is an incentive beginning at 100 per cent productivity in which the percentage increase in wages is equal to the percentage in savings in hours over standard hours. This has been known as the Rowan Plan and bonus earnings can never exceed the base rate (Fig. 14).

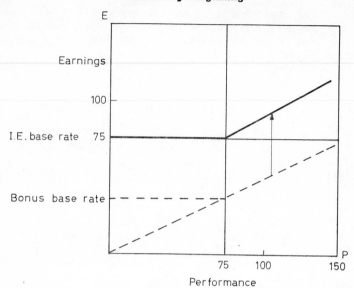

Fig. 11

DIRECTLY PROPORTIONAL INCENTIVE ON ONLY PART OF THE BASE RATE

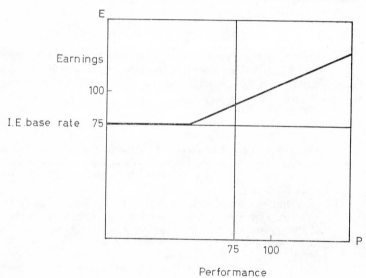

Fig. 12

LESS THAN DIRECTLY PROPORTIONAL INCENTIVE STARTING AT LESS THAN
75 PER CENT PERFORMANCE

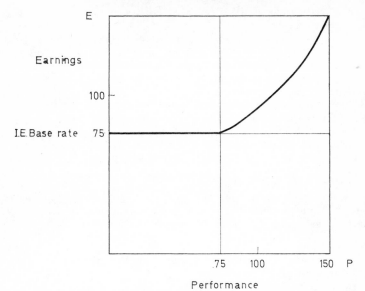

Fig. 13 Accelerating Geared Incentive

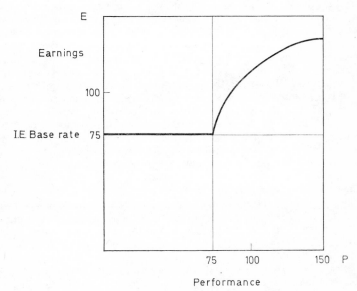

Fig. 14 Decelerating Geared Incentive

The relationship of (i) to (vi) need not be continuous but may be in a series of steps.

There are generally further complications relating to the basis of payment for waiting time, unmeasured work, experimental work, etc. Perhaps the most important of these is waiting time. There is the usual balance of argument between paying for lost time at the IE base rate and paying at the average of recent incentive earnings. If lost time is poorly paid, the tendency will be for the operatives to put pressure on the management to eliminate the cause of lost time—it is taken for granted that the incentive scheme will discourage the worker from wasting time himself. Against this is the reasonable argument that if the lost time is not the worker's fault, why should he lose money as a result. The further counter-argument is to the effect that incentive rate of pay can only be paid for an incentive rate of working. Often a compromise is reached and lost time is paid at some rate between IE base rate and the incentive earnings rate appropriate to 100 per cent performance.

PROS AND CONS OF SCHEMES PROVIDING REWARDS BASED ON
WORK MEASUREMENT

Payment-by-results schemes have been very adequately ventilated in the Prices and Incomes Report No. 65. The area in which there has been most controversy in recent years has been in the rewarding of individual workers for performance based on work measurement. As with so many areas in the industrial relations field, it is possible to muster arguments and facts to support quite adequately diametrically opposed viewpoints. It is also generally impossible to find an ideal solution—each solution contains a mix of advantages and disadvantages and hence has to be tailor-made to the specific situation.

It is generally unpopular or considered old-fashioned to argue in favour of work measured incentives. Yet where the worker can substantially influence output it is difficult to understand why. The important satisfiers have been demonstrated by Herzberg to be the opportunities to take responsibilities, to achieve, to obtain recognition and to reap the reward of advancement. Incentive schemes provide two of these at least—the opportunity to achieve and obtain recognition. They are not inconsistent with the other two, which management should think about and introduce into their industrial relations policies via training, job enlargement and worker development schemes. The other telling point is the experience that where they are appropriate, incentive schemes generally produce higher rates of working than when they are absent.

Where are incentive schemes inappropriate? Clearly they are inappropriate where the workers cannot affect the output rate in any significant way. Also, where optimum worker effort is not really required, work measurement on its own may be enough to achieve a satisfactory rate of working. Incentives bring enough trouble in their wake that no-one should think of using them unless the potential cost of dealing with these difficulties is going to be out-weighed by the opportunities and advantages. This situation usually occurs where workers can substantially affect the output and utilization of machines or other expensive productive resources.

The design of an incentive scheme based on work measurement requires a greater degree of skill than is generally recognized. To be adequate, such a scheme must be a reasonable (mathematical) model of what takes place at the machine or work area and must take account often of complicated interactions of men and machines. Such schemes have historically been introduced by consultants using staff of high calibre and experience. When they have left a company, the staff left behind to maintain the schemes and design new ones have generally been of a lower calibre and experience and, as the years have passed, the numbers of these have frequently been allowed to dwindle, and the morale of the time study and incentives group has begun to fall.

Frequently also, the introduction of time-studied incentives is done without the very substantial training and consultation that is necessary at all levels of management but particularly at the supervisory level. In consequence a situation tends to arise where supervisors and, often, production management as a whole, regard the whole subject of incentive schemes as something which is administered by the time study department (which by this time has often been linked to the wages office).

At worst, the time study staff become isolated and production management appear to make concessions, ignore over-booking, fail to ensure schemes are worked properly and the morale and numbers of time study staff fall further. This is perhaps an extreme but not unusual situation.

It is from this position, with schemes having become slack, with uneven earnings potential on different schemes and with a multitude of human relations problems, that an alternative basis of motivation is sought.

If this stage is reached it may well be the best solution to move to an entirely new basis, and change, in itself, is often beneficial.

However, it is not inevitable and universal that time studied incentives deteriorate. It is in the nature of all incentives and controls that they tend to slacken under pressure from those to whom they apply, but adequate numbers and calibre of time study staff together with full production backing and participation can ensure continuing maintenance and liveliness for such schemes. Some of the advantages and disadvantages of incentive schemes based on time study are briefly:

Advantages	*Disadvantages*
Generally effective in producing a high rate of working.	May cause deterioration in quality.
Limits need for supervision.	May inhibit improvements in method.
Helps to ensure that prescribed methods are used.	Causes much negotiation over details. With slack schemes may limit output.
	Supervision is more difficult.
	Does not encourage a feeling of participation.

LARGE GROUP SCHEMES

THE RELATION BETWEEN EARNINGS AND PERFORMANCE

With large groups, the same variety of relationships between earnings and performance as exists with small groups is possible. In practice, the types (ii) and (vi) are most usual (p. 51). Sometimes some method of smoothing payments is introduced, so that some proportion of high bonuses is held back and added to low bonuses.

PROS AND CONS OF LARGE GROUP REWARD SCHEMES

Compared with individual or small group schemes, large group schemes have the advantage that they encourage co-operation within the group and the disadvantage that because the individual contribution is not individually rewarded, the incentive effect is more diffused.

The work of craftsmen in particular is often such that it requires co-operation. One worker, if motivated to skimp his job, might increase the amount of work for the following trade. As members of craft unions are frequently opposed to the principle of individual incentives, group incentives are widely used with this type of worker. Where individual incentives have completely deteriorated, where technical factors make it difficult to measure work accurately, where labour relations are at a particularly low level, where there is considerable demarcation of jobs and where, as so often happens, several of these factors are present simultaneously, then some form of group incentive scheme is likely to improve the situation.

Group schemes, reflecting as they do the work of the group, provide the need and the means for consultation over a wide range of topics affecting the productivity of the group. Furthermore, the larger the group the more realistic are the effects of change in productivity (on which most of these schemes are based) on the overall costs and efficiency of the company. In contrast, the small group or individual schemes only relate to productivity at a machine or work place, the effect of which may be lost, for example, by production delays, machine breakdowns, etc.

Some group schemes do not provide any absolute measure of productivity (as at least in an approximate way, work measurement schemes do) but enable changes of productivity to be measured. This means that the level of productivity before a scheme is introduced clearly influences the potential increase in productivity that can be expected. Where the initial level of productivity in absolute terms is not known, it is prudent either to use a shallow relationship between earnings and productivity or else to use a geared relationship.

SYSTEMS BASED ON PENALTIES

Systems based on penalties are not considered likely to be of substantial importance in areas where there is acute labour shortage.

Perhaps the most important consideration for the future applies to some measured day work schemes where the arrangement is made that workers may be down-graded or even dismissed if, after a fairly exhaustive procedure of examination of work, measured times, method of training, the worker consistently fails to achieve a required standard.

Otherwise penalties can often effectively and acceptably be tailored into small group reward type schemes to ensure that increased output is not obtained at the expense of some other desirable factor such as high quality, low fuel consumption, etc.

It is usual to design the schemes to combine penalties for three or four reasons. As the expression 'penalty' although descriptive of the scheme, is generally quite unacceptable to employees, it is usual to avoid the term and many so-called 'group bonus schemes' do, in fact, have a substantial penalty element which is not drawn to people's attention.

Nevertheless, penalty schemes are often effective and acceptable to the work people and easy to run, in the fairly limited number of circumstances in which they can be applied. They may be more easily understood and liked if referred to by the colloquial expression 'Chinese Doctor Schemes', the origin of which is the historical story that doctors in China were paid only when their patients were fit and well. A maintenance team for an important machine might be paid maximum bonus when it is running, and lose all bonus when there is a breakdown.

This is clearly fair, although the men are paid least when they have to work hardest. The 'Chinese Doctor' type of scheme is ingenious and often successful where it can be made to capture the imagination of the workers concerned.

Factors used as a basis for penalty schemes include:

Orders on which losses are incurred.	Scrap.
Orders delivered late.	Overtime worked.
Yield.	Complaints received.

SYSTEMS BASED ON LEADERSHIP AND PERSUASION—
MEASURED DAYWORK

These schemes are based on the principle that the main motivation of workers should spring from their own sense of responsibility, persuaded and led by supervisors who are skilled in human relation and man management techniques and provided with adequate control, information and statistics. As applied to the shop floor this approach is frequently termed measured daywork, and consists of paying the workers at a full bonus rate (high day rate) and in consequence expecting a good day's work at bonus rate of working. The work is measured in one or other of the ways described under 'Work Measurement' (p. 14) and the results of the measurement are made available to worker and supervisor. If the work measurement results show a lower performance than is regarded as satisfactory then the worker and supervisor attempt to discover the reason, with the responsibility for doing so on the supervisor.

In consequence, the decision whether to use such a scheme depends on an assessment of the ability of supervision and the sense of responsibility of workers.

One situation where the approach has proved successful has been where productivity of the workers is low, and where the achievement of a normal day rate of working represents a considerable improvement over previous performance. This is the situation which exists in many indirect areas and where often payment by results would be socially unacceptable.

Another situation where the approach has been successful has been where much of the work is machine-paced and where a good pace of work has already been established.

If systems of this type can be made to be successful, a number of substantial advantages result:

    i. Ideas and suggestions are encouraged from the shop floor.

    ii. Resistance to change on the part of operators is substantially reduced when their earnings are in no way affected by the change.

    iii. There is no urge for employees to 'conceal' methods improvements in order to have something in hand for a bad day.

    iv. Work study engineers can devote more time to methods, instead of being burdened with the administration and arguments connected with an incentive scheme.

    v. The 'atmosphere is more conducive to the running of an effective suggestion scheme.

    vi. Measured daywork provides a sound basis for supervision: foremen have to use their supervisory authority, because they cannot sit back thinking that the incentive scheme will secure the necessary output for them.

vii. Labour relations are improved. One reason for this is that workers do not have an 'incentive' to question all 'standard times' and argue about them.

viii. Worker flexibility is improved. It becomes easier to get people to take on the new job, or the awkward one, because workers do not lose money when they leave the task to which they have become accustomed.

ix. Standards can be revised more easily, so that the steady 'deterioration' normally associated with conventional incentive schemes should not occur.

x. There is less paperwork.

xi. Over a period of time, the status of the supervisor is improved.

There is little doubt that measured daywork can represent a very enlightened way of organizing work so as to ensure effort, but in areas accustomed to piecework which are only partially or not at all machine controlled, it would appear that very considerable preparation should be undertaken before introducing it.

RUCKER AND SCANLON PLANS

The basic idea behind these plans is the same although the details and calculation may vary according to the firm or the industry concerned.

The starting point is the argument that for years there has been a 'battle' between management on the one side, and workers on the other. In effect, the workers have been trying to get a bigger and bigger share of the available money, and they want this paid to them as wages; meanwhile the management have been trying to get a bigger share, with which to pay staff salaries and shareholders' dividends, increase capital investment and hold down prices as costs rise. Both 'sides' have wanted a bigger share of the 'cake'.

The idea behind these schemes is that in advance, the management negotiates a 'formula' which determines how big the two shares should be. Thereafter it is to both sides' advantage to 'increase the size of the cake' because this is the only way that either party can get more money.

When management and work people are pulling together rather than fighting each other, it is possible for productivity to be increased substantially.

There have been many successful applications of this idea. It originated in the U.S.A. and in Canada, but there are numerous successful examples of schemes in the U.K. Similarly, there have been failures, so the idea is not a panacea to cure all ills.

The most effective basis for such schemes is to guarantee the work people a given proportion (say 38 per cent) of the Added Value of a company, which is defined as 'The Sales Value of Output less the cost

E

of materials, power and sub-contract services'. This appears simple:

$$\frac{\text{Wages paid to hourly paid employees}}{\text{Sales} - \text{Materials, etc.}} = 0.38$$

but in practice quite complex accountancy is involved.

Surprisingly the ratio at any given firm remains very nearly constant for many years, but much investigatory work has to be carried out to see what it is. For example, the 'Value of Sales' may be known, but the 'Sales Value of Output' may necessitate more accurate recording of value of work in progress, fluctuation in stock, etc., than is usual. Similarly 'Wages paid to hourly paid employees' sounds straightforward but there may be staff people doing work jobs, and people on the clock doing staff jobs.

It is necessary to reveal rather more of the company's figures than is usual in the U.K. (i.e. monthly turnover, cost of materials, wages) but it is not necessary to reveal the profit. The scheme is *not* a profit sharing scheme, and it is possible for employees to earn bonuses when the company makes a loss, and for employees to earn no bonus when the company makes a profit. Nevertheless, there is an element of sharing, so the employees' earnings are reduced when the company has to cut selling prices to get business.

It is usual to guarantee the employees their earnings based on normal union negotiations plus national awards, with the proviso that if productivity is increased, a monthly bonus will be paid out if the actual earnings fall short of those calculated on the agreed ratio. Three-quarters of the surplus is paid out monthly, the remainder being kept in hand for 'bad months' and if not so required, is paid out as 'holiday' or 'Christmas' bonus.

Whilst the principle is quite opposed to conventional ideas, the success of numerous applications makes such plans worth more investigation, and trial if a suitable location can be found. However, the following points should be observed:

(a) Widespread publicity is needed—since there are no 'teeth' in the plan, it will not work unless it is put over enthusiastically and continuously.

(b) Timing is important. As employees share in the company's misfortunes as well as in their good times, the plan must not be installed just before a slump.

(c) There must be a reasonable mutual trust between management and workers. One negotiates on the basis of indeterminate 'percentages' rather than measureable things like 'minutes' or 'pence', so the employees must believe in the integrity of management in preparing the accounting figures on which the scheme is based. (Some firms permit outside auditors to represent the unions.)

EXAMPLE OF THE RUCKER PLAN

Over a period of five to six years the results shown below have been obtained.

	£
Net Sales	12,750,000
LESS External materials, supplies and services	5,370,000
Production Value...................	7,380,000
Factory Wages	1,900,000

Ratio of Wages to Production Value.... $\dfrac{1,900,000}{7,380,000} \times 100\% = 25.7\%$

In a particular month, after the Rucker Plan has been accepted and a ratio of 25.7% is in use:

	£
Net Sales	520,000
LESS Change in work in progress (at Sales Value)	40,000
Sales Value of Production	480,000
LESS Materials and Supplies	196,000
Production Value	284,000
Factory Wages Actual.................	70,000
25.7% of Production Value	73,000

Hence saving (comparing actual wages with what would have been expected in the base period) available for distribution to the workers
$$= £73,000 - £70,000 = £3,000$$

THE SCANLON PLAN

Also American in origin, this has a less rigid set of rules than the Rucker Plan, but it does have a basic formula. This relates labour costs to sales value of production and uses this ratio to determine any saving in labour costs, which forms the bonus. Sometimes all the bonus is distributed to employees, though some firms keep 25 per cent and distribute the rest. The base ratio is less stable than that of the Rucker Plan, as it can be affected by the introduction of new machinary or substantial prices.

EXAMPLE OF THE SCANLON PLAN

Applying the same values used in the previous example of the Rucker Plan, the base period figures are:

	£
Net Sales	12,750,000
Factory Wages	1,900,000

$$\text{Ratio of Wages to Sales} \ldots\ldots\ldots = \frac{1,900,000}{12,750,000} \times 100\% = 14.9\%$$

In a particular month, after the Scanlon Plan has been accepted and a ratio of 14.9 % is in use:

	£
Net Sales	520,000
Change in Work in Progress (at Sales Value)	40,000
Sales Value of Production	480,000
Factory Wages Actual	70,000
14.9% of Sales Value	=71,500

Hence saving (comparing actual wages with what would have been expected in the base period)—this is available for distribution to the workers:

$$= £71,500 - £70,000 = £1,500$$

5

Preparing for Productivity Bargaining

THE PRESSURES FOR PRODUCTIVITY BARGAINING

There might be some organizations which provide for a productivity bargain as part of a long-term plan. As sophisticated forward planning gradually becomes the rule rather than the exception, as companies examine the likely development of their products and markets, consider the impact of competitors' product and market changes, assess the demands on and the probable supply of various categories of manpower, so the number of productivity bargains conceived as part of an overall company mid- or long-term plan will increase.

For some considerable time, however, the norm will be the productivity bargain which is produced as a result of some form of direct or indirect pressure. Even the best planning contains a large element of forecasting and there will always be unforeseeable changes in market and product which give rise to unexpected changes in technology and manpower. These will lead to pressures which might well result in a decision to embark on a sectional or comprehensive productivity bargain as quickly as possible.

The 'pressure' which has led most companies into productivity bargaining has been the wage claim or the threatened wage claim. Before the days of Incomes Policy, most companies would have overcome the problem by embarking on the game of finding out the lowest figure at which the unions would settle; usually there was little attempt to assess what, if anything, was really due. Provided the numbers involved in the initial claim were small, management's conscience was eased, for they did not have to think of a large sum in settlement. The fact that one conceded claim led to another might not have escaped their notice, but it made life very difficult to work out all of the possible repercussions of a claim and many companies lacked the expertise to do this. There was a certain fatalistic response to claims which was based on the assumption that regular increases were inevitable on one pretext or another, and it did not matter very much whether consequential claims were foreseen or not.

The great change which the years after 1966 brought to British industry was the acceptance that there could be no worth-while wage

63

increase without an increase in productivity, and that it was not only advisable to be aware of the consequential effects of any wage increases; it was a duty to assess them accurately and take them fully into account when balancing the cost of an award against the productivity returns. The acceptance of this change has been neither complete nor voluntary, but that the philosophy is now firmly established is evidenced by the number of genuine productivity deals which started life simply as pressure for higher wages.

Other pressures which prompt productivity bargaining include extreme demarcation and flexibility/mobility of labour problems. For many years there seemed to be no way through these intractable defensive barriers until productivity bargaining showed that there was a way, because restrictive practices can be listed and the benefit to everyone of their removal can be demonstrated. This was first widely publicized in the Fawley productivity agreements. The Fawley agreements have been criticized for erring too much on the side of 'buying out' restrictive practices. It is right to be cautious of directly 'buying out', and it is certainly now fashionable to criticize the Fawley agreements, but at least there is now an established method of tackling restrictive practices with some likelihood of success.

Less directly, a productivity bargain might be prompted by a company's inability to attract the quality of labour it requires, which on examination it finds is due to paying wages which are low in comparison with the district average. It might once have remedied the situation simply by raising its bid in the labour market, thus solving one problem at the expense of another, for its competitive ability must have suffered in consequence. Such a company will now usually seek ways of recovering the cost of increasing its wages bill and must inevitably consider the productivity bargain. Examples of other pressures which can precipitate productivity bargaining are loose incentive schemes, the awareness of lack of effort in the workplace, and a deteriorating competitive position which directs attention to excessive unit costs. Even productivity bargains themselves can generate pressure for productivity bargains in other companies. This has given rise to the criticism that the increased wage rates cause unfavourable comparisons to be drawn in other companies, which are thus placed in an embarrassing position. Those who voice this criticism have short memories if they suggest that this did not happen before productivity deals were the vogue, and they fail to grasp that, unlike past wage increases, those resulting from productivity bargaining are justifiable on explicit grounds.

Whatever the particular pressures might be that cause an employer to embark on productivity bargaining, it is probable that at a very early stage he will have formed some idea of the complex problems involved in such things as wage structures, productivity measurement, work measurement, and incentives. What can very easily be taken for granted is the amount of preparation needed, the length of the negotiations which will be entailed, and the full extent of the additional demands on management throughout all the stages of a deal. If any of these points are under-estimated it may not be just a disadvantage at a later stage, it may well ruin a productivity deal even before it gets off the ground. If, for instance, the pressure prompting a productivity deal is a wage claim, a company will be in real trouble if it does not think out, and spell out for the benefit of the Unions, the length of time it will take to implement a bargain and consequently to pay the increased rates.

PREPARING THE GROUND

One of the authors has a favourite story: 'My first married home was one of a pair of newly-erected bungalows. My neighbour, a fastidious gardener, set out to make a lawn. He levelled the ground and sifted and rolled the soil; then he re-levelled, re-sifted and re-rolled until September came and went and he decided that it was too late to sow the seed. The following spring he started on the levelling, rolling and sifting cycle again and in fact he rolled, levelled and sifted his way through the four years I lived there. Visiting the area three years later I called on my ex-neighbour and asked how the lawn was going. "Very well," he said. "I've just finished sifting the soil and tomorrow . . ." '

The story is related here because what follows is a counsel of perfection, and it is as well to recognize now that striving for perfection when preparing the ground for lawns or productivity bargains, will mean that a start is probably never made or, at the very best, the risk will be run of missing the sowing season and the possibilities of success will gradually diminish. On the other hand, disaster is courted if the preparation is skimped. Between the two extremes is an accepted standard of preparation which (for productivity bargaining) will include much, if not all, of the following.

TOP MANAGEMENT

Everyone will accept that top management support is essential. It must, however, be active and understanding support and not just a formal expression of encouragement. The Board—or whatever the top management of a company may be called—must know and appreciate the reasons for embarking on a productivity bargain. They must not simply think that it is a 'good thing' but must be convinced that it would be unreasonable for the company to do anything else. The first task, therefore, is to establish to the Board's executive members a prima facie case for a productivity bargain. Once this has been done they can be told just how demanding the exercise is going to be on their time. From beginning to end—from initial preparations to full implementation and beyond—these people are going to be continually involved and they will reduce their involvement only at the peril of the productivity bargain. Some members of the Board will obviously be more involved than others, but comprehensive productivity bargaining covers so many facets of the business that it is unlikely that any members will escape some of the extra load.

The involvement of the Production Director and the Board members responsible for Personnel and Management Services is obvious; but the Financial, Sales, Engineering and Technical Directors will all be involved because of their particular responsibilities:

the collation and checking of existing and proposed costs of production and labour,

estimating the effects of increased volume on deliveries and assessing the extent to which increased production resulting from increased productivity could be sold,

the provision and cost of maintenance cover for increased machine utilization time,

the desirability of introducing technical changes and methods of increasing technical efficiency to match increased productive efficiency.

The list is not complete but it is long enough to leave no room for doubt on the involvement of *all* Board members, including the Managing Director.

Apart from their specialist interests, the Board will be concerned with the overall benefits and changes to the company which a productivity bargain will bring. They will themselves be caught up in change: the need to think in terms of the company's objectives and of their own key tasks; new systems of exercising their control overtaking older methods which might not have been adequate for a long time but which have never been questioned. The biggest change of all will be the acceptance that successful productivity bargaining is dependent on willingness to share information on the company's products and operations which hitherto might well have been confined to the Boardroom. So much information on organizations is public knowledge anyway and so much is prey to elementary deduction. Of the rest, there probably never was a decent reason for calling it confidential except that people often feel at an advantage if they are privy to information which other people do not possess.

The danger of useful information falling into competitor's hands is the commonest reason given for keeping information confidential. It is not suggested that this danger is non-existent but it is often grossly overplayed; for example one Financial Director refused to discuss the annual accounts with Shop Stewards for this reason, and as the accounts were already published, it is sad to reflect that the company's competitors were thus better informed than the representatives of its employees. If there is a genuine readiness to share most of the relevant information with Shop Stewards, there will be no problem in withholding that very small proportion which really could be of interest to a competitor.

Several companies already provide access to the sort of information which should be offered to employees' representatives at the productivity bargaining table. However, to most Boards this will be one of the major changes in attitudes which productivity bargaining will call forth, and unless these changes in attitude at the top are accomplished, the scope of the productivity bargain will be restricted. (The Fairfields' productivity bargain probably had its greatest advantage in this respect. It started off under an entirely new management, uncommitted to the past and mindful that the Unions were already in full possession of facts, figures and forecasts.)

If there is a good reason to avoid giving profits in £ *s. d.*, some other acceptable yardstick of measuring the company's present and future performance in this respect will have to be devised, but it always has more impact to quote actual money values. The commonest reason for not talking profit to employees is the fear that they will consider it excessive and will press wage claims. Very few British companies generate excessive profits and very few therefore have good reason for not discussing this information. If managements do keep quiet about such things they have only themselves to blame if the wrong interpretations are put on this by their work people, who can be excused for assuming that profits must be so excessive that they should keep on lodging claims until they have soaked up the surplus. How much better to deal in fact rather than fantasy, to let employees know what profit levels are and to guide them in understanding what they could be and should be.

Once the Board is convinced of the need for a productivity bargain, and recognizes the changes in attitude demanded, it has three immediate tasks:

   i.   to allocate the broad responsibilities for mounting the operation;

   ii.   to fix a rough timetable and arrange to monitor progress;

   iii.   to review its specialist resources and decide what additional help is needed either to meet the target date or simply because the company does not possess a particular expertise.

The allocation of the broad responsibilities for mounting the deal will be eased if there are specialist Personnel and Management Services Directors. In a large group of companies it might even be possible to second such people to the Board for the duration of the deal.

If these specialist functions are not represented at Board level, the Board will have to decide which of its members should have prime responsibility for which phases or parts of the operation. In a small organization, one member might cope with the complete bargain from beginning to end. It will usually be more advisable to nominate two members, one to concentrate on the personnel aspects (industrial relations, negotiations, communications, redundancy and redeployment, etc.), and one to oversee the industrial engineering side (measurement of work and productivity, incentive schemes, method study, etc.). There will in practice be a considerable amount of overlap (e.g., wage levels and rates). Both members will be responsible for reporting progress to the Board, explaining difficulties, reviewing priorities, and ensuring that the Board is totally conversant with and committed to each of the several steps as they are taken.

The Board, under the guidance of the one or two members mentioned above, must next examine the resources within the Company to determine whether they are adequate for the tasks ahead. Again, if there are established personnel and industrial engineering (or work study) functions the task will be eased, provided they are operating at a reasonably expert and senior level.

If the Personnel Department is simply a collecting house for hourly-paid applicants and if its members are predominantly visitors of the sick and arrangers of pensioners' parties, it will be far better to keep as great a distance as possible between them and a productivity bargain. What is required is a Personnel Department which is well organized, capable of producing sound policies and used to guiding and controlling industrial relations and wage and salary structures. In addition, the Work Study Department should be concerned with something more sophisticated than rate fixing and should already be regarded as the main source of advice on incentive schemes and methods. If a company has people of the right calibre, however, it must next decide whether it has enough of them. If there are not enough of them is there time to add to their numbers?

Companies might get concerned at this stage at the prospect of an embarrassing surplus of specialist staff when the productivity deal is all over. It is worth bearing in mind that a productivity bargain from beginning to tried-and-tested operation will probably extend over two years and the wastage rate of qualified and experienced specialist staff could well indicate that additional staff at the beginning will mean normal manning at the end.

If it is decided that internal resources are not going to be sufficient, a company must look for outside help. If the company is part of a large group it might be possible to get people on secondment, but the most likely source of outside help will be management consultants. In reality, even those firms with well-established Personnel and Industrial Engineering Departments have had to call on consultants for at least some of the work connected with a productivity bargain. Those organizations without specialist personnel and industrial engineering facilities will probably have no alternative. They might, incidentally, consider it an opportune time to establish these functions. The people who staff the new functions might not be able to contribute significantly to the bargain, especially in the early stages, but they will have an exceptional opportunity of building up rapidly their knowledge of the company and the implications of the bargain and will thus provide valuable continuity when the consultants have gone.

If consultants are to be engaged, the Board, under the guidance of those of its members specifically responsible, must define precisely what the consultants will do. They must not be told simply to 'do a productivity bargain'; they must specifically be told their tasks and a realistic timetable should be agreed for the completion of each major task, e.g.:

Task	Programme
Assess present operator performance and indicate potential improvement.	Week 1.
Prepare job evaluation proposals, discuss and agree methods with managers and shop stewards.	Week 2.
Undertake job evaluation of all hourly-paid jobs and agree final gradings (not rates) with shop stewards.	Weeks 3–28.
Prepare training programme for departmental managers and all supervisors.	Week 4.
Implement agreed training programme for above.	Weeks 8–28.

If a Board does not do this, it must not be surprised if its consultants follow their own ideas, do work which could be done (or has already been done) by the company's own people, and take much longer in doing all of this than a company can afford both in terms of money and time.

It is the company's responsibility to maximise the productivity of its consultants. The cost of consultants should be looked on as an investment and for this reason alone a company will choose its consultants with care in order to ensure a good return. Inexpert consultancy can leave in its wake a trail of problems which can take years to put right, particularly if industrial relations have been impaired. A Board must therefore examine the credentials of the consultancy organization it is thinking of using, will check the reputation of its principals and will ensure that it is known to have experts in the work the company wants done. It will also ensure that the company will have the services of these experts throughout the assignment; some consultants have a tendency to replace their experts with somewhat less experienced people after the first few days of the assignment. Much useful information both on the work which needs to be done and on the ability of the consultancy organization itself, will come from the initial study that the prudent company will ask for.

Advice on consultancy organizations and their particular fields of expertise can be obtained from a number of sources. Employers' associations will often be able to help (the Engineering Employers' Federation, for instance, has a Director of Advisory Services who is able to give guidance to member companies). The British Institute of Management also has collected a great deal of information on a number of consultancy firms. Most of the information collected by such organizations will relate to the large or medium sized consultancy companies but small consultancy firms should not be overlooked: they might be marginally cheaper and, more important, the assignment may well be directly supervised by one of the principals.

It is also possible to retain a consultant who will help a company to select the consultancy organization most appropriate to its needs, to establish terms of reference and make regular progress checks on the work of the consultancy organization chosen. His role is thus similar to an architect's and, like an architect, he can very easily save many times the cost of his fee.

Attention has already been drawn to the extent of the involvement of top management and the time it will have to devote to the productivity bargain. This additional load will be reflected in other levels of management and the participation and varying interests of so many people can obviously lead to fragmentation and duplication of effort and also to the danger of leaving undone things that ought to be done. To meet these problems it will usually be advisable for the Board to appoint a senior manager to co-ordinate the work that goes into a productivity bargain. This 'co-ordinator' might be a specialist or a line manager; he must have a sound general knowledge of the company and must have an understanding of matters such as industrial relations and work study. He should be named at the earliest stage— probably on the recommendation of the Board members with particular responsibility for the bargain—and he should be relieved of all, or substantially all of his normal duties as soon as the initial work commences.

Between being named and starting work he should familiarize himself with the technique of productivity bargaining and its implications. Useful methods of building up a background knowledge include attending short but comprehensive courses, visiting companies which have completed bargains, talking to employers' organizations and the Department of Employment and Productivity and studying relevant publications such as those given in the Bibliography.

The existence of a co-ordinator will not only ensure that all things are done when they should be done. It will also remove much of the detailed progress-chasing from top and senior management and enable them to devote more time to their particular responsibility and the overall strategy of the bargain.

The Board must give consideration to one further matter before its initial tasks are complete. As a productivity bargain progresses, certain people are going to become key men. An obvious example is the co-ordinator, but there are others who will become closely associated and closely identified with the bargain. Some, like the co-ordinator, will be apparent before the deal gets under way, others will emerge as key men as the work progresses. At the very least, the loss of one of these key men would be an embarrassment and would result in some delay. A more probable effect is that some of the benefits to the company envisaged in the proposal-forming or negotiating stages, would be overlooked or allowed to lapse in the implementation of the bargain. It is important that the key people are retained, at least until the productivity bargain is part of the accepted day-to-day life of the organization. The Board must, therefore, make sure that these people, as they are identified, are not likely to be tempted away.

THE PREPARATION OF LINE MANAGEMENT AND SUPERVISION

The whole-hearted contribution of this group is vital. This sounds so obvious, yet it is probably the area most often quoted by managements when listing the errors and omissions in their productivity bargains.

Front-line supervisors in particular can make or break a productivity deal, especially in the formative and negotiating stages, simply by the way they respond to questions and comments on the proposals from their shop floor operatives. They do not have to have any intention of sabotaging a deal to break it. If they do not know what productivity is all about, if they do not know the company's particular aims and the reasons for them, and if they do not know their part in the pattern and how the bargain will affect them, there is a good possibility that they will seriously impede progress on the deal. An agreement might be made without their total involvement, but a company will not reap the full benefits it ought to obtain when the deal is put into practice.

The uninformed and uninvolved supervisor is unlikely to make a constructive comment on his company's productivity bargain. If he is forced to make some comment he may well cover up his ignorance with some non-committal remark which will arouse suspicion in the mind of his questioner.

From the earliest stages, line management and supervision have got to be able to talk knowledgeably and convincingly to the shop floor, to give authoritative answers or know where they can get the answers quickly. They have got to exhibit confidence in the deal and in the people devising it. If this happens, they can not only 'make' a deal, they can in certain circumstances save it. If, for instance, the Union channel of communications from the negotiating committee through shop stewards to the shop floor fails, the supervisor's role in passing on information to the operatives, answering their questions and allaying their fears, becomes vital.

All of this means an extensive and continuing training and communications exercise with line management and supervision from the principles and philosophy of productivity bargaining in general, through to the implementation of a productivity bargain in the particular.

At the earliest possible stage, very soon after the Board has completed its initial tasks, these people should be taken into the confidence of top management and asked for their views and ideas on how productivity might best be increased and how this is best put over to the shop floor. This will be done by group discussions and individual interviews; the use of 'mechanical' aids such as the printed management survey questionnaire is also valuable. An abbreviated example of such a survey is given at Appendix 3.

A full survey is much longer and, where a large number of supervisors and managers is involved, computer help will be needed to analyse the results. Some of the information obtained from the analysis will not be new to the management but, if the survey is properly devised and conducted, some surprises are guaranteed. It is usual and understandable for top management to be hesitant about using a survey; there is predominantly concern that the supervision might object to answering some of the questions or even to filling in the form at all. Experience shows that the reverse is true. Employees, and particularly those in responsible positions, almost invariably welcome the opportunity of stating their views and stating them frankly.

Having gone to so much trouble to get the views and opinions of line management and supervision, and to get them feeling involved in the exercise, it would be galling to forfeit their interest and goodwill by failing to keep them adequately informed of the progress of the deal. The manner in which this is best done will depend on numbers, on the size and spread of the factory, and on existing communications media. The command channel of communications—from the Board, through the various levels of management to front-line supervision—should be the major means of passing and seeking information. This should be supplemented by regular meetings of groups of supervision and the distribution of short summaries of progress and problems. The frequency with which all of these means are used will build to a peak as the proposal forming is completed and negotiations get under way.

The effort and time that must be devoted to line management and supervision is thus considerable, but it will be more than repaid, not only in terms of the productivity bargain but in an improvement in the attitude and contribution of this group to all aspects of their employment with the company.

A factor which will affect the attitude of front-line supervision is the extent to which they will benefit from the productivity bargain. If a company is going to emphasize—as emphasize it must—the value and importance of their contribution, and if, as is probable, the bargain will demand considerable change in the working methods and habits of the supervisors themselves, it is inevitable and reasonable that they should expect some tangible benefit. It is suggested that the same principles should apply to money increases for the supervisors as applies to money increases to the men, i.e. that the amount of the increase should be justified by the extent of their contribution. The method of applying the increase will depend on the present policies and practices of the company—although these may need revision—but will depend also on how and when their contribution is made.

A method which has worked well in some companies is to establish a percentage differential between the supervisor and the average or upper quartile earnings of workers in the factory. The supervisor gets his increase as soon as his department changes to the productivity bargain basis and his salary is reviewed every three months or so during the period that earnings are rising. Thereafter he would revert to a six-monthly or annual review.

Whatever the supervisors' increase and however it is paid, it is a reasonable cost against the benefits of the productivity bargain and should be shown as such when the scheme is finally submitted to the Department of Employment and Productivity.

There is often a temptation to delay talking about supervisors' increases until the negotiations with the unions are complete. It is a temptation to be strongly resisted, for even if a company can talk only in terms of general principles instead of actual cash, it will make a tremendous difference to the spirit of the supervision in the early stages. The main reason for this will not be the carrot of additional money, but that the management has given thought to their interests and has not taken their expected contribution for granted.

THE PREPARATION OF THE SHOP FLOOR

In deciding how to tackle this, much will depend on the strength of union representation among the people involved. Numerical strength must be assessed but this is not always an accurate indication of the true strength of the Union. How influential are the senior shop stewards and the department shop stewards? How much confidence has the membership in them and in the local and national union organization? Will the rank and file do as their representatives recommend, or will they only do so when it suits them? Front-line supervision will often be able to give sound answers to these questions. The attitude survey (mentioned more fully below) will also give useful indications of the health of the trade union body. Shop stewards themselves will sometimes be prepared to be frank and open on these questions once they are sure the company intention is to be constructive and not exploit any weakness revealed. If there is a significant trade union membership, it is in the company's interests to ensure that it is well organized and well represented, for it must be recognized that the additional strains introduced by productivity bargaining are proportionately as great for the unions as for the management. If there is any inherent weakness in the trade union structure, there is a very real danger in the negotiating stage that the structure will collapse. If this happens it will be to the detriment of everyone in the company. Not only will the productivity bargain be shelved, but a hiatus will develop in the day-to-day negotiating situations.

How then does a company set about correcting weaknesses in its trade union structure? The identification of specific weaknesses will often suggest the cure. General 'flabbiness' might be helped by better facilities for the Union or by Shop Steward training. The local union official will usually be a source of advice and help, and he has the added advantage of being able to make suggestions to the domestic trade union circles with less likelihood of being viewed with a jaundiced eye.

Having ensured that the trade union structure is going to be strong enough to cope with productivity bargaining, shop floor preparation will centre on shop steward preparation. These representatives must be given internal and external training in the principles of the productivity deal, in the techniques of negotiation, and in methods of keeping their constituents informed. The constituents themselves should have the opportunity of attending regular departmental meetings with supervision, but the company's efforts in their direction can, if necessary, be limited to ensuring that the trade union channels of communication are working effectively. It is in any case worth bearing in mind that too much emphasis on communicating directly with the shop floor might, in a highly union organized setting, lead to suspicion of the managment's motives.

If trade unionism within the company is so weak as to be virtually non-existent, and if no other official or unofficial system of representation exists, the management must take the initiative in establishing some acceptable form of departmental representation. A joint consultative or joint productivity committee with representatives elected by ballot, is a possible solution. Much of the preparation of the rank and file for the advent of productivity bargaining can then be done through the medium of these committees. A great deal of work will also have to be done within each department, mainly by meetings between the management, supervision, and operatives, to make sure that every operator understands, or is given the opportunity of understanding, the philosophy of productivity bargaining, and later, its practical application to their own situation.

Attitude surveys carried out on all or a sample of the work force are a valuable source of information on such matters as the effectiveness of communications systems and the satisfiers and dissatisfiers in employment conditions. They can also demonstrate a surprising preparedness for change and will thus often indicate that a company can be much more adventurous in its productivity and wage proposals than it might otherwise have thought. A further important benefit of the Attitude Survey is the sense of involvement it engenders: employees know that their opinions, views, and suggestions are being taken into consideration in the formulation of the proposals.

An abbreviated Attitude Survey is shown at Appendix 4.

PREPARING THE COMMUNICATIONS NETWORK

Communications are never perfect, but in most companies they are just about good enough to rub along in normal circumstances. Productivity Bargaining, however, is not 'normal circumstances'. It imposes exceptional strains on the communications systems, and it is consequently important to overhaul these systems and eliminate or get round obstacles.

The biggest obstacle to good communications is the desire not to communicate. This will often be found somewhere in the command or 'line' channel, which is the most important of all. The reasons for not wanting to communicate stem sometimes from the tenet that subordinates should not expect to have information passed to them— that they should 'know their place'—and sometimes from the sense of superiority derived from knowing something that other people do not. Whatever the reasons, it is important to identify the blocks and find some way of circumventing them—it will not usually be possible for the leopards to change their spots. The command channel of communication, like most things, will improve with use and it is up to the senior echelons of the company to show that they expect it to be used by meticulously observing it themselves. It is especially important that they should be on their guard against by-passing the command channel; supervisors will often complain that they do not see enough of the Managing Director on the shop floor, but woe betide him if he stops to answer an operator's question while he's there.

Joint consultative systems are a valuable aid to communications. There must, however, be a parallel system of discussion with line management to provide a prompt 'feed' from the consultative into the command channel of communication.

A lively consultative committee can be a useful sounding board and source of ideas when a productivity bargain is being planned. It can be a useful aid even in normal times. Critics of joint consultation will say that it often degenerates into 'tea and toilets' but even the critics will accept that management calls the tune and if management does not

F

guide the consultative committee towards the things that matter, it must expect it to revert to trivia.

It must be acknowledged that consultative committees have in the past had their own rapid obsolescence built into their structure. Managements have, for example, insisted on free elections of representatives, often taking pains to emphasize that this was a matter quite outside the union's sphere of influence. The result was that most, if not all, of the consultative committee members held no union office and might not even have been members of the union. As a consequence, the management would tend not to discuss any important matter with the consultative committee because it realized that this would at best only be an academic exercise and at worst, might interfere with subsequent negotiations. If an important matter were raised by management, the representatives, being conscious of their non-representative negotiating position, would either be non-committal, or would give the company a totally erroneous impression of the reaction that would be encountered in negotiation.

The answer which many companies have adopted is a virtual fusion of consultation and negotiation. The representatives on the consultative committee should be shop stewards who will not only be prepared to discuss important matters authoritatively but will encourage the company to raise the important matters to begin with, thus preventing any possibility of degenerating to tea and toilets. The advantages of this system are threefold:

   i. The company is consulting with the people who will be negotiating.

  ii. Shop stewards are much more open and constructive in the consultative situation than in negotiations.

 iii. Both parties have the opportunity of exploring each other's views free of the tensions of the negotiating situation.

If a company is considering productivity bargaining and it does not possess a system of joint consultation, it must decide whether to manage without or whether there is time to set something up. It must be borne in mind, however, that a consultative committee must be given time to find its feet before being subjected to the strains of the productivity bargaining situation. Therefore, unless a company is planning well ahead, it is probably safer to leave the introduction of joint consultation until after the negotiating stage. Provision for joint consultation can in fact form part of the company's productivity proposals.

Publications, such as company news-letters or magazines, are useful ways of publicising and creating informed interest in the productivity bargain. Regular summaries of the up-to-date situation sent to supervisors, and the judicious use of notice-boards, are even better ways of using the written word.

PREPARING THE GROUND: OUTSIDE BODIES

i. EMPLOYERS' ASSOCIATIONS

If the company is a member of an Employers' Association, the earlier preparations should include a visit to their offices to outline the company's plans. There was a time when this might have been courting trouble. Employers' organizations were by and large so reactionary, so very much the prisoners of established practices and procedures, that any attempt at rational discussion on a comprehensive productivity bargain would probably have been doomed, and there was an outside chance that the company might be under some pressure to drop the idea. Some firms deemed it prudent to leave their employers' organizations before embarking on a productivity bargain. Such actions, and the influence of the Government and the Prices and Incomes Board, hastened the wind of change and, in the course of a year or so, a marked change occurred in the philosophy of most employers' organizations. These central organizations in effect accepted that workplace negotiations had long-since supplanted national bargaining as the means of establishing earnings levels. Industry-wide negotiations would in future concentrate on basic conditions and procedures, and on guide lines for effective plant bargaining. The local associations were encouraged to adopt the role of supporters—almost promoters—of meaningful plant agreements.

If employers' associations are to play this role effectively, there is an obligation on the constituent employers to submit their proposed agreements to the local association for vetting. It is thus a duty to consult the employers' organization at the earliest stage of a productivity deal, but it is a duty that employers will accept willingly whenever they are sure that they will get constructive and encouraging advice. Employers' organizations have some way to go before they are making their fullest contribution to their new roles, but the speed with which they have begun to adapt themselves to modern conditions and outlook bodes good for British industry, especially if the trade unions are stimulated to follow their example.

There may be local associations which are still run by people who do not see the need for change. Employers served by such an association should remember that it is their job to press for changes, and in the meantime should take their productivity proposals to the national organization or to the Confederation of British Industry. The C.B.I. in fact is also willing to help firms which are not members of employers' organizations.

ii. THE DEPARTMENT OF EMPLOYMENT AND PRODUCTIVITY

There is perhaps still a temptation for some employers to shudder at the thought of civil servants dabbling in business matters. Ministry of Labour officials never quite measured up to the popular conception of civil servants, however; their work exposed them to the facts of industrial life and over the years they have assembled a great deal of knowledge of the problems and opportunities facing industry. The prospect of using this knowledge to better advantage, presented by legislation and other Government effort, has been welcomed by them with enthusiasm, and in the field of productivity bargaining in particular they have displayed a grasp and insight which many consultants cannot emulate. This fount of knowledge will usually be found at the local Regional Headquarters, and an employer will be doing himself a dis-service if he does not consult them in the exploratory stages of a deal and also at the proposal-forming stage. He is bound to consult them before the deal can be finalized, as we mention later on.

iii. LOCAL UNION OFFICIALS

It is wise to let them know as soon as the decision to start work on a productivity bargain is made. This gives the company an opportunity to assess the local official's reaction and gives the local official a chance to prepare his message for the shop stewards when they consult him. It is particularly important to establish this contact with the local officials if the ability of the domestic union organization to deal with the bargain is suspect. As mentioned earlier, he might well be able to help prepare the shop stewards for their task and he will also give some indication of the circumstances in which he would be willing to take a more direct part in negotiations. Some employers' organizations will insist on one of their officers being present at any discussions between a member company and a union official. If the employers' organization concerned is sympathetic to the notion of productivity bargaining, the presence of one of their officials could well be of some advantage. If the employers' organization is unsympathetic, the presence of one of their officers will obviously inhibit discussions and will militate against the establishment of the rapport which is being sought. It is up to the company to classify its own employers' association and decide whether to involve them in this stage or not.

PREPARING THE GROUND: THE NEGOTIATING SYSTEM

All companies have negotiating systems of some sort which cope with varying degrees of effectiveness with the claims and disputes which are part of industrial life. The negotiations entailed in productivity bargaining are, however, quite out of the ordinary. They will be lengthy and arduous and will demand a lot of continual 'homework' on the part of the negotiators to keep up with and assimilate the wealth of detail which must inevitably be introduced. A company must therefore critically examine its present system and judge the extent to which it will measure up to the stresses of a productivity bargain.

In most cases it will be found necessary to set up a special negotiating committee, especially if more than one union is involved. The membership of such a committee would probably be on the simple basis of the senior shop steward from each union involved, with perhaps additional weight for any union with a large numerical superiority, matched on the management side by senior executives or directors from production, personnel, and industrial engineering functions, plus the co-ordinator if he is not represented under another hat. The right 'mix' will vary from company to company.

There might sometimes be resistance to the idea of all the unions concerned negotiating as one body. Such resistance might come either from the unions themselves, or from management circles, who might either see some tactical advantage in splitting the unions up, or fear the consequences of them working together. Comprehensive productivity bargaining, however, involves everyone, each group having its contribution to make and having its effect on the other groups. There is thus an overwhelming argument for one comprehensive negotiating committee, which from the beginning should help to promote the inter-union understanding and co-operation so often lacking in companies.

Having decided on the basic negotiating machinery, a company must next look at ways of resolving problems which the negotiating committee might disagree on. There will probably be an industry procedure for settling matters outside the company, but this should be subjected to the same critical examination as the domestic procedures before accepting it as the best way of settling productivity bargaining questions.

Most industry disputes procedures take a long time to complete and, if a company is well on the way to implementing a productivity bargain, it will not welcome a sudden delay of two or more months. One answer is to agree with the unions on the appointment of an arbitrator who will be prepared to deal speedily with any matter referred to him. When drawing up these negotiating procedures for its productivity deal, a company would be prudent to provide for the worst possible eventuality and build in an agreed cooling-off period in the event of a serious breakdown in negotiations.

PREPARING THE GROUND—CONCLUSION

At the beginning of this chapter we recognized the danger of appearing to counsel perfection. The company which covers thoroughly all the stages of preparation mentioned will come near to perfection, and will be something of a phenomenon. Most companies will cover much of the ground, but they will be trying to run a business at the same time as preparing a productivity bargain. For this reason alone some of the areas will not receive the thorough attention which, in the ideal situation, they should. Furthermore, productivity bargains have a tendency to develop their own momentum, which it might be undesirable to restrain, and are susceptible to sudden increased pressures, such as an upsurge in the demand for the company's products, which, without the deal, would demand additional labour. It is obviously not feasible to delay everything while each stage of preparation is completed.

However, if a company has prepared a check list of the sort of preparatory stages mentioned here, it will have the positive advantage of being aware of the areas which it has not been able to prepare adequately, and it will thus be ready to respond quickly to any signs of difficulty in those areas. Given this sensitivity to potential danger spots, the worst effects of any under-preparation should be averted.

6

Preparation of the Survey and Developing the Wages Structure

There are often two stages involved in the preparation of a productivity bargain. The first is the preparation of an outline deal. This involves a preliminary assessment of the potential value of expected productivity improvement and the likely costs of the changes in the wages structure necessary to release the potential. If this first stage discloses that a reasonable opportunity for a successful bargain exists, then the second stage can be proceded with.

This usually requires some form of job evaluation and analysis of present wage rates. From this, and a variety of proposals concerned with bonus payments and allowances, a pay structure can be built as a basis for the initial negotiations. This combined with many other aspects discussed in Chapter 5 enables the Productivity Bargain documents to be drafted.

ASSESSMENT OF POTENTIAL BENEFITS AND COSTS

The main sources of benefit for the firm are:
    improvements in rates of working,
    reductions in the number of indirect workers in relation to output,
    improvement in productivity,
    improvement in added value,
    reductions in absenteeism and labour turnover.
There may be other benefits which are thought to be available. These should be identified and the present level and expected improvement evaluated.

The methods used to evaluate some of these factors are now discussed.

ASSESSMENT OF RATES OF WORKING

The assumption is made here that work-studied incentives are already installed, and that there are varying degrees of slackness. It is important to realize that in most firms no one knows the true rate of working. A good deal of information is produced in many companies showing the weekly performance of workers but on most of the schemes (and therefore at most of the work places) the actual rate of working is not known. It is only where a scheme has been re-assessed recently, or a new machine has been introduced and work studied values have been put in for the first time, that the true rate of working is available. The reason for this is that, over a period of years, the value of a standard minute in a work studied incentive scheme depreciates. After five or ten years a standard minute may be worth only half of what it was originally. Consequently, a 100 BS performance may be recorded as 200 or more.

In order to understand the complete position in a company a detailed survey is required which lists the various incentive systems, the wage rates and performances.

DETAILS OF SURVEY OF INCENTIVES

The information required for each incentive scheme is as follows:

    i. number of personnel involved
    ii. whether the scheme is an individual or small group scheme or whether it is a large group scheme
    iii. whether the scheme covers direct workers, indirect workers, or maintenance or craft workers
    iv. the form of the incentive
    v. the base rate or minimum fall-back rate
    vi. the relationship between performance and bonus
    vii. the manner of calculating the actual bonus
    viii. the effect on bonus of 1 per cent change in performance of the individual.
    ix. the performances being achieved as being recorded by the company (using B.S.I. scale)
    x. the performances being achieved as obtained by actual shop floor assessment (B.S.I. scale)
    xi. fluctuations in performance over a six-month period
    xii. the number of clerical hours per week to operate the scheme
    xiii. some notes on the effectiveness of the scheme
    xiv. the date when the scheme was last revised.

For the indirect workers (except those linked directly to incentive schemes) a different procedure is used involving activity sampling or some form of labour scheduling. The object is to assess the number of indirect workers required in various departments. It may be possible, if time is available, to assess the probable effects of method improvements in arriving at these manning levels. For the maintenance workers, activity sampling can also be used if agreement can be negotiated with the appropriate unions and there will usually be no difficulty if incentives are already in use in these areas. Where there is no previous history of incentives, it is generally not unreasonable to assume that a substantial potential is available for improving productivity.

Information is then summarized for each department and for the direct, indirect and craft workers, under the following headings:

i. number of people on incentive
ii. percentage on incentive
iii. money paid as bonus per worker per week for those on incentive
iv. percentage bonus to gross wage
v. the average hours worked for the gross pay
vi. the average rate of working as recorded by the company (B.S.I. scale)
vii. the average rate of working as found from careful actual assessment (B.S.I. scale)
viii. the average real S.M.s produced per week
ix. the average percentage of unmeasured work
x. the average percentage of lost or ineffective time
xi. the method of payment for unmeasured work and ineffective time
xii. the method of payment for rejects and re-works
xiii. the methods of checking accuracy of values and bookings
xiv. the average wage of those not on incentive
xv. the average rate of working of those not on incentive
xvi. the cost of actual S.M.s produced.

In the outline deal preparation stage, the above assessments may be done approximately or on a sampling basis. Subsequently, in the preparation of a negotiable wages structure, the more detailed investigation and assessment is necessary.

PRODUCTIVITY AND ADDED VALUE

Productivity and added value can usually be assessed from historical records.

As to productivity most firms have weekly or monthly historical records of total labour clock hours and of output measured in some way. This enables a preliminary assessment to be made of the historical level of productivity. It also reveals whether soundly based productivity relationships can be established on existing data or whether it will be necessary to require new information to be collected and summarized.

Added value can usually be assessed with reasonable accuracy from monthly trading statement results, if these are prepared. An assessment will also be available from the annual results. The latter assessment is likely to be more accurate but the monthly figures disclose the possible variations.

Forecasts of possible improvements in productivity and added value depend on improvements expected in rates of working, reduction of indirects, reduction of lost time, reduction of rejections etc. The components of productivity and added value and forecasts of improvements should be listed. The value of these improvements can then be estimated.

The value of reductions in absenteeism and labour turnover can also be assessed in terms of their effect on productivity.

DEVELOPING THE WAGES STRUCTURE

If the preliminary outline calculations indicate that a productivity bargain is economically feasible, then the first stage will probably be to proceed with job evaluation.

JOB EVALUATION

The first stage, as mentioned in Chapter 4, is to discuss with representatives of the workers the principles involved and the methods to be used in job evaluation. It is essential to get this understanding, because very much is going to hinge on it later on in the development of the bargain, and in the operation of the bargain in future years.

The second stage is the appointment of a main Job Evaluation Committee, consisting of management and employee representatives. The first task of this committee should be to issue, for general information, a document stating:

    i.   the principles of job evaluation,

    ii. how it works,

    iii. how the assessment procedure will be organized as between the management and the workers,

    iv. what procedures will be made available to settle differences between managers and the workers' representatives.

    v. procedures to settle differences between the Job Evaluation Committee and an individual worker.

The task of the Job Evaluation Committee is to complete the evaluation of all jobs according to the method chosen. If the grading method of job evaluation has not been chosen, the committee might be charged with putting evaluated jobs into grades. Otherwise, this—and the agreement of money values to the grades—might be left to the negotiating stage of the productivity bargain. The management representatives on the committee will usually include people from production, work study, engineering, and personnel. The workers' representatives will be drawn from shop stewards. The Job Evaluation Committee should have some permanent members and some that vary from department to department. The permanent members are important in order to ensure continuity of standard and interpretation throughout the whole job evaluation procedure. The members that vary will be the manager and the shop steward in each successive department.

RELATING THE JOB EVALUATION RESULTS TO THE TOTAL HOURLY RATE

As a result of the work previously described there is available a substantial table in which the average rate of working of each job is listed together with the total hourly earnings. From this it is possible to calculate what the total hourly earnings would be at 100 BSI rate of working. This is a considerable task but it is an essential preliminary to a proper assessment of the present position of the company and the potential for improvement.

Assuming that a points rating method of evaluation has been used, it is now possible to plot a graph, with the job evaluation points along the x axis and the total hourly earnings at 100 BSI rating plotted on the y axis. (*See* Fig. 15.)

If a point is put on this graph for each job, the result will be a scatter diagram. A regression can be calculated through this scatter diagram which represents the average relationship between total hourly earnings and job evaluation points. This can be done on a departmental basis and comparisons made between departments.

The scatter of the points on this diagram is a picture of the anomalies and difficulties in the present wages structure.

THE WAGE STRUCTURE

What is required is to establish a new wages structure which will be simple to understand and to administer, and which will meet the specific needs of the company.

The desired wages structure should have a limited number of grades —often as few as five or six. The total hourly wage grade levels should not be excessive in relation to the district, but it is important that they will be sufficiently high to attract the types and grades of labour the company requires.

The cost of the new wage grades should not be out of line with the benefits which the company can obtain from the workers in terms of increased productivity.

The steps from one grade to another should be reasonably even. In other words, if the wage grades are drawn on the diagram as they are in Fig. 15, the series of steps should be fairly regular in pattern.

It is an advantage if the information about wage rates for the various jobs and the job evaluation results can be put into a computer programme. A wide variety of arrangements of wages structures can be simulated, enabling the cost to the company and the benefit to any class or group of worker to be assessed. Having the information on a computer also enables the management to respond quickly to suggestions for alterations which will doubtless come up during the negotiating stages.

There is no doubt that the rationalization of the wages structure will cost money, and consideration has next to be given to the means by which this can be recouped.

The strength and amount of incentive to ensure the realization of benefits has to be a compromise between the motivational effect of

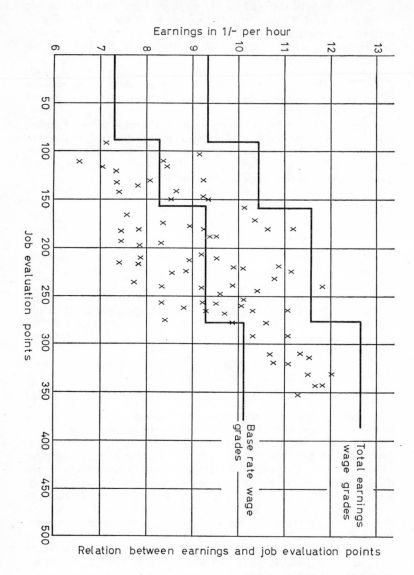

Fig. 15 RELATION BETWEEN EARNINGS AND JOB EVALUATION POINTS

the incentive and the danger of inequalities arising between one group and another and thus destroying the rationality of the wages structure. This part of the exercise can best be illustrated by an example:

The XYZ Company thinks there is considerable scope for improvement in the direct worker rate of working and effectiveness. The direct production workers are already accustomed to individual incentives. Part of the deal will be the reassessment of the existing incentive scheme. It is therefore agreed to propose a reasonably strong incentive for the direct production workers to increase their individual and small group effort and effectiveness. Accordingly, a bonus will be defined for the 100 BSI level. The direct workers will also participate in a departmental group bonus scheme such that they obtain a defined bonus if the department in which they work achieves the target level of Departmental Productivity.

For the indirect workers it is recognized that it is not appropriate to measure their individual effort and accordingly, it is agreed that they should be able to earn a defined bonus, if the department in which they work achieves the target level of Departmental Productivity.

For the maintenance and craft workers it is proposed that they participate in a factory-wide bonus based on productivity and machine availability.

A periodic revision of the base rate is to be made. This will be based on the labour proportion of the total added value in the company for the period concerned.

Such a pattern of incentive payment is designed and consideration is given to developing the base rate structure from the previously designed structure of wage rates at a 100 BSI performance. Consideration also has to be given at this stage to allowances for shift work, overtime, holiday pay etc.

A series of detailed calculations are involved at this point in order to establish a reasonable base rate structure. Although the wage structure at 100 BSI performance is ultimately what is going to decide whether the workers think the scheme is a good one or not, it is the structure of basic wage rates, allowances and incentives that will attract most attention in the negotiations.

7

Formulating, Negotiating and Implementing the Productivity Bargain

THE FIRST DRAFT

Throughout the preparations, investigations, and discussions mentioned earlier, information and ideas will be accumulating from which will eventually be drawn the components of the productivity bargain. The co-ordinator will have ensured that, as it arose, each bit of information, each set of statistics, each suggestion, was discussed and evaluated with the senior executives and directors concerned, and that the more significant items were considered by the Board. The co-ordinator will have collated this mass of information and it is his job now to sit down and assemble in one 'package' the draft productivity and wages proposals. He will have to call on the various experts concerned with the proposals to assist him with, and possible to write up, the sections which fall within their particular spheres of interest.

In this first draft the aim is to put together the proposals and supporting evidence in some comprehensible sequence. Editing, style and grammar can be left to the final draft. First should come the aims of the company in proposing a productivity bargain, how it seeks to achieve those aims, and what the achievement will yield. Next will come a statement of what the company believes the employees want from a productivity bargain, how the company proposes to meet these needs, and what they will cost. Finally will come any additional matters which, although not necessarily part of the bargain proper, it is nevertheless desirable to include. Examples are proposals for setting up joint consultation machinery and the company's policy on redundancy.

From the first word of the first draft the company will be conscious of the fact that it is writing words which will be read by the opposing negotiators. There will be numerous temptations to withhold certain information, to mask the true effects of some of the proposals and to overstate on the employees' gains. It might indeed be tactful to omit some of the information which does not have any real bearing on the fundamentals of the bargain, but it is tactics and not tact if information which is germain to the productivity bargain is withheld simply because it might enhance the opposing negotiators' ability to argue their case.

These tactics are, furthermore, doomed to failure, for sooner or later the true facts will emerge and, when this happens, the company's intentions will look even blacker than they really were.

It is undeniable that in the past both sides of industry have distorted or concealed information to suit their own case and that this is an accepted practice of industrial negotiation. It is also true that it is difficult to change the pattern in the normal everyday run of negotiations. Productivity bargaining, however, is not the same as normal everyday negotiations. It is different enough to provide the very opportunity for which all ought to be seeking to make a break with the cloak-and-dagger practices of industrial negotiations. Its scope, its rewards and its implications are potentially so great that, in any case, the risk of justifiable accusation of bad faith on either side cannot be entertained.

There is therefore more than one reason for meticulously ensuring that, from the preparation of the first draft onwards, no significant piece of information is obscured, that none of the implications of the proposals is concealed, and that as a result the whole document will ring with straightforward, untarnished and unchallengeable fact. This does not of course mean that none of the facts will be challenged in the subsequent negotiations. It does mean that, having challenged some facts and found them not to be wanting, the great mass of the document will justly be accepted at its face value. Conversely, if one fact is found to be erroneous, suspicions will be aroused and every fact, every figure, will be checked.

While he is writing up the proposals, the co-ordinator should bear in mind that, because he and his colleagues have been involved in the detailed collection and preparation of the mass of information produced, it is easier for him to understand than for anyone reading the document for the first time. It will be doubly difficult for shop stewards, most of whom will never have been faced with a remotely similar situation. It is important therefore to ease the task of comprehension by simplifying the content as far as practicable and by giving short explanations of any techniques or technical terms mentioned. In addition, it is advisable to preface the document by a summary—a bird's eye view—of what is asked and given in the proposals.

The emphasis on frankness should be extended to include clear acknowledgements of the difficulties which might be encountered. If it is likely that something in the proposals will arouse opposition from, say, a union district committee (and it will be surprising if something doesn't) then this should be stated. It goes without saying that a sympathetic statement recognizing their problems in adapting to a changed situation but emphasizing the advantages of the change, is likely to have more effect than a reference to any inbred reactionary tendencies.

District committees are likely to exercise more influence as plant and local bargaining becomes more the vogue. Provided they recognize that the best interests of their members are served by improving the efficiency and productivity of the firms in their district, this need not be a bad thing for the employers. Indeed it could be that they would offer better leadership and control than many full-time officials have demonstrated in the past. Whatever the advantages or disadvantages of the future it is as well to recognize that district committees will have some comments to make on a unionized company's productivity proposals. If a company states that it foresees difficulties with a district committee there is the prospect of criticism being drawn into the open. Such open criticism is less likely to be ill-informed, emotionally prejudiced and non-constructive.

RELATED COMPANY POLICY

When the co-ordinator has drafted out the components of the bargain proper, thought should be given to the desirability of including some statements of company policy on related subjects on which people might be hazy—and consequently suspicious. Redundancy policy is an obvious candidate, even if no redundancy is expected to result from the proposals, for it adds considerably to an employee's sense of security if he knows how he will fare in the worst possible event. Policies governing up-grading and promotion, discipline, dismissal and appeals procedures, and the treatment of employees in the event of long-term ill-health, are other associated subjects. If these things are known and written down already it is perhaps sufficient to list them as references. Including these additional related matters has the added advantage of presenting a clear image of the company as a body prepared to communicate positive attitudes (and in communicating, to invite discussion). This image of a mature, progressive company is important not just for the company's employees but also for local union officials, the D.E.P., and district committees, who might know next to nothing about the company. Productivity bargaining is an opportunity to improve the company image internally and externally, and if the image is improved externally the morale is improved internally.

When the co-ordinator has completed the draft and it has been agreed, someone whose written English is notably clear and concise should go through the document. This will not only improve the style and clarity, but might also reduce the length by 10 per cent. The proposals are then ready for their public showing.

PARTICIPATIVE PROPOSAL FORMING

The method of proposal forming described above is virtually a management exercise. There is another method which could be called participative proposal forming. In this, representatives of the work-people are involved from the earliest stages.

If there is a well-established and effective system of joint consultation, and the consultors are also the negotiators, the company could use this to discuss its productivity problems and discuss ideas and eventually draw up proposals. Alternatively, the company, having decided that there could be scope for a productivity deal, might set up a negotiating committee which, after piloting through job evaluation would consider various aspects of productivity bargaining in depth and gradually develop proposals. Separate sub-committees may be set up to deal with different topics, possibly prompted by 'discussion papers' prepared in advance by the company or the consultants advising it. Participative proposal forming, however it is done, demands a more positive industrial relations background than the pure management exercise, and it takes time to get shop stewards talking freely and frankly about demarcation, shift-working and such things. The whole process of proposal forming takes much longer but it could well be that the negotiating stage is considerably reduced, since most of the arguments and explanations will have taken place. Participative proposal forming could give an increased sense of commitment to the eventual agreement on the part of the shop stewards, as they themselves will have been involved in the origination and development of the agreement. It is important that throughout such an exercise the line management and supervision are kept involved and informed, and particularly that they are aware of, and have an opportunity to comment on, the proposals that gradually take shape.

If a company decides to develop its productivity bargain by a union/management participative process it is worth considering whether discussions should be prefaced by the publication of a joint 'Statement of Intent'.

STATEMENT OF INTENT

A productivity bargain is unlikely to succeed without the full support, commitment and enthusiasm of all parties concerned. There has to be the firm intent to make the bargain work and a well thought-out Statement of Intent made at the right point in time can often assist the development of a productivity bargain.

A Statement of Intent can cover principles, responsibilities, safe-guards, ends and means. It can also cover the reasons for change.

An Introduction is useful to list the parties to the statement, the subject matter to be covered and any historical event(s) which initiated the discussions etc. leading to the Statement. It might also list the main headings to follow.

G

Example:

1.1 This Statement of Intent is made by the XYZ Company and by the members of the A.B.C. Union at the XYZ Company.

1.2 This Statement refers to the principles to be followed in developing a comprehensive Productivity and Pay Agreement between the XYZ Company and the members of the A.B.C. Union. It also sets down the responsibilities, safeguards and the main steps which it is intended will be taken.

1.3 This Statement follows discussions between the Management of the XYZ Company and a negotiation committee of the A.B.C. Union, which was set up subsequent to the one-day token strike on . . .

1.4 It is agreed that (i) the present wage structure contains anomalies and makes the recruitment of some categories of labour difficult; (ii) the present system of incentives needs to be revised and reconsidered; (iii) there is considerable scope for increasing productivity.

The statement of principles may cover points such as:

increased productivity should be rewarded by increased pay;

any restrictive practices (whether by Management or Workers) should be eliminated;

Workers and Management pledge themselves to do all in their power to increase productivity; (This may be amplified.)

the methods to be used to measure productivity both for individuals and small groups, will be fully understood and mutually agreed;

Messrs. D.E.F. Management Consultants will assist in the preparation and implementation of the Agreement.

Their Terms of Reference will be mutually agreed.

Responsibilities will include communication—an important joint responsibility of both management and unions. It follows that there are responsibilities in setting up adequate communications machinery. Management responsibilities include providing adequate staff, paying the consultant's fees, providing facilities for discussions, preparing the documents necessary for the Agreement, devising the administrative machinery to operate the Agreement, and so on. The union responsibilities are to be fully aware and to understand all that is proposed and to make proposals themselves. The union can also help substantially to create an atmosphere of enthusiasm and co-operation with a concentration on opportunities.

Safeguards include subjects such as security of employment, wage rates during the preparation of the Agreement, time allowed to prepare the Agreement, renunciation of the use of pressure during negotiations, provisions for resolving disagreements, training workers' representatives, access to information, etcetera.

Ends and means might outline in the broadest possible terms what it is hoped to achieve and the means to be used, e.g. more productive and better paid workers, equitable wages structure, shift working, the use of the techniques of job evaluation, productivity measurement, incentives, method study and formalized cost reduction.

It is as well for the Statement of Intent to be as brief and simple as possible. It should not read like a legal document and there should not be too great an endeavour to make it completely watertight. It should rather aim to create an ambience of optimism, enthusiasm and co-operation throughout the company.

The signing of the Statement of Intent should be given adequate publicity. It can be reproduced in booklet form so that every employee has a copy. Everyone then knows what is going on and what is expected of him.

If a company chooses to produce its productivity proposals as a management exercise it must accept that it cannot do this 'publicly'. The proposals must be treated as confidential until the document is finally presented. If an effort is not made to avoid premature disclosure of information there is the danger that a disjointed version of one or other of the proposed changes will circulate in the company. This could upset industrial relations and perhaps necessitate the exclusion of the true version of the change from the final proposals. To avoid this sort of eventuality the company must restrict its deliberations and drafting of the productivity proposals to a relatively small and senior management team. This unfortunately means that line management and supervision cannot be included, although their thoughts and reactions to various ideas will already have been canvassed thoroughly as mentioned earlier.

PRESENTATION OF THE PROPOSALS

When the document is complete, copies of it must be given to everyone involved in a negotiating, supervising or related role. If the proposals have been arrived at by a participative process this will be a simple administrative task. If however the proposals have been developed as a management exercise, careful thought must be given to the manner and sequence of distributing copies. The following pattern will be suitable in most cases.

   (a) Senior managers meet their line managers to distribute copies of the proposals, discuss in confidence the contents and describe the procedure for announcing the proposals, negotiating, and keeping line management and supervision informed.

(b) When the line managers have had an opportunity of digesting the proposals (and at least a day should be allowed for this), they should see their foremen and chargehands and repeat the exercise with them.

(c) At about the same time the local officials can be met by the personnel manager or similar official and copies of the document can be handed to them.

(d) Finally, a meeting should be held with the senior shop stewards to discuss the proposals briefly and hand them sufficient copies for themselves and any other major shop stewards. At this meeting the proposed negotiating arrangements will be discussed and the stewards should be asked to request the first negotiating meeting as soon as they have had a chance to study the proposals in detail.

It is possible that some 'reflex' response will follow within a matter of hours and one or more shop stewards might want to start talking—virtually negotiating—particular points. Every effort should be made to persuade them to take more time to study the whole document carefully and this is a useful opportunity of re-emphasizing that the proposals cannot be lifted out and treated as separate entities but are inter-related and interdependent.

At this stage the company should be prepared for some exposure to the Press. Productivity bargains are likely to be news—if only local news—for some time to come and it is important that the company knows what it wants to say and agrees this with the unions involved. Most companies are notoriously shy of press mentions on such matters. They will happily spend large sums on advertisements which are seldom read but will stand resolutely in the way of this sort of publicity which has much more impact and can do more good for the company image, the importance of which has already been stressed. Employees like to see their companies making the right sort of news. A company will recognize this to its advantage and will perhaps consider that good publicity of a productivity deal could well enhance a man's pride in his company and might even predispose him to making the deal work. If on the other hand he reads that 'the company refused to comment' he is not likely to be swept off his feet in admiration for his management and could even have his suspicions aroused. He might question that if the company really is doing something good, why should it be afraid of publicity.

Finally, at the stage of announcing the proposals, a company should let its neighbours know what it is doing so that they can talk knowledgeably if they have claims for their own employees. It would be unfortunate if one of them rushed to increase its rates simply on the information that this is what one of the companies was doing 'down the road'.

NEGOTIATION

At the outset of the negotiations it should be made clear that, if more than one union is involved, the agreement cannot be concluded until all unions have accepted the proposals.

The method of negotiations—either the existing system, the existing system with modifications, or a special negotiating committee such as that described earlier—will be detailed in the proposals which now constitute a negotiating document. The important thing for the negotiators to bear in mind, from the time they first sit down together, is that they are embarking on a new negotiating situation which represents an opportunity to break with the customary cloak and dagger style of negotiations. The management team must take the initiative on this and demonstrate from the beginning that it is prepared to put all its cards on the table, must explain how the sums are done and must have all the supporting information ready to produce if it is asked for it. The negotiators on the other side will take a little while to get used to this and to reassure themselves that everything is as above-board as it appears, but they will respond in like manner given time. The management team must resist the temptation to withhold certain information or 'whitewash' their case, and must, above all avoid being 'clever'. The odd tactical success might be momentarily satisfying but it will not help their overall strategy, for the truth will emerge eventually. It might be helpful if they openly acknowledged this in the hope that the other negotiators recognized that it applied equally to them. The company might well emphasize their point by making it clear that if any decision and agreement is based on incorrect or misleading information the whole matter is open to renegotiation. It is worth remembering that one of the major potential benefits of productivity bargaining is not written down in the proposals: it is the improvement in the whole industrial relations sphere which follows from the better understanding, trust and more positive identification with the enterprise which gradually develops round the negotiating table.

As the negotiations proceed there must be regular report-back sessions with line management and supervision so that they in turn can talk knowledgeably to the shop floor. In so doing they can check that the union channels of communication are working properly. If they are not working properly, the fault must be found and corrected quickly. Possibly a meeting of all shop stewards will suffice, possibly meetings involving all of the work people will be needed. There will in any case be occasions during the course of the negotiations when the negotiating shop stewards should be allowed—and encouraged—to hold such meetings, at which the local full-time official could usefully be present. Such meetings are costly in terms of company time, but the number of meetings and the length of them need not be great, and the cost would be that much greater if ignorance were allowed to persist and grow.

When all of the initial negotiating hurdles have been overcome, the negotiating committee should devise and issue to all employees a booklet setting out the main points of the proposals. Brevity and simplicity must be the keynotes of such a publication and a question and answer style is probably the most effective.

Negotiations are likely to be long and pressures will be great on all the negotiators who must be on their guard against 'negotiating fatigue'. Top management can contribute greatly at such a time by showing that it appreciates—indeed expects—the difficulties and is nonetheless still committed to seeing the deal through to a successful conclusion. If difficulties are such that they cannot be resolved by the negotiating committee, the local union officials should be asked to assist. Where several unions are involved it may be that only one or two are holding up progress. In such an event a meeting of the local officials, without the management present, might clear the problems. In the extreme case the industry negotiating procedure or the arbitrator, if one has been appointed, should be used, but this step should be very much a last resort.

It might be that negotiations are foundering because of the difficulty of appreciating the full actual effects of the proposals. If this happens, it is worth going to some trouble to set up a pilot scheme in one department or area. This can demonstrate what the proposals mean in terms of changed methods and conditions and in terms of new earnings against current earnings.

Eventually, given patience and goodwill, negotiations will be successfully concluded and the productivity proposals will become a productivity agreement. At this stage the company should be ready again to meet the Press and should quickly produce the agreement in booklet form for all of its employees.

D.E.P. APPROVAL

The approval of the Department of Employment and Productivity must be obtained before the payment proposals of the agreement can be put into effect. It is suggested that the proposals are submitted to the D.E.P. when negotiations are well advanced—probably at about the same time that the short 'question and answer booklet is prepared for the employees. If the proposals have been well constructed with an eye to the Prices and Incomes Board criteria, and the D.E.P. advice obtained in the preparatory stages has been followed, there should be no problem about their approval. The proposals can of course be submitted to the D.E.P. before they are presented to the unions—and it is wise to do this if the company has any doubts or reservations—but in most instances it is preferable to delay the submission until the first round of negotiations has produced its crop of changes. The majority of changes will be made in these early stages and there will thus be very few on which to consult the D.E.P. after their approval has been obtained.

The D.E.P. will require a complete set of the pay and productivity proposals, summarized to show how these meet the P.I.B. criteria. They will need a few days to study the documents and will then wish to discuss them and probe the background thinking and the bases for the various calculations. Their examination is searching and the examiners are well-informed, but they are also sympathetic and any advice they offer will be constructive.

A week or two will elapse before the D.E.P. give their answer. This will be either 'approve', 'not object' or 'not approve'. In the first two cases the company can go ahead with its deal, though it might be worth while looking at the reasons for the qualified approval implicit in the second grading. If the proposals are not approved, reasons will be given. As stated earlier this is a most unlikely answer if all the previous steps have been assiduously followed.

IMPLEMENTATION

The implementation of the many changes inherent in a comprehensive productivity agreement will take time. Where work measurement throughout a factory is involved, either for the first time or as a re-assessment, it may take twelve months or more in a medium sized concern. Consequently, some form of interim award might be appropriate to bridge the gap between acceptance of the proposals and their application to all workers, particularly those at the end of the implementation queue. Pressure for an interim award will be greater if wage rates are already below the average and, if this means that the company is having difficulty in recruiting and retaining employees, it could be that such a payment is in the company's interests.

The efficacy of money as a motivator depends largely on the potential gains available to the worker. In more colloquial language— there must be something to go for. The difficulty in making interim rewards is that they erode the potential financial incentive.

One way of avoiding this erosion is available where part of the bargain is to pay some bonus related to departmental productivity. This can usually be measured quickly, particularly where specialist help is available aided by computer analysis. The interim award can then be the departmental productivity bonus.

Another interim arrangement that is frequently employed is that of an introductory allowance. This is a means of overcoming the natural caution of the worker when faced with a new bonus scheme. It provides him with a safeguard, usually by guaranteeing or making the achievement of a given level of bonus easier, for a defined period. Introductory allowances are a traditional feature of many bonus schemes

and are often valuable. It is, however, essential when introducing such
an allowance to establish the period of time for which the allowance
will stand and the arrangements for removing it when its useful life
is finished. A progressive reduction in the amount of the allowance or
guarantee is a usual method and this must be clearly stated at the
outset. If this is not done, it will prove difficult to remove the introductory allowance. There will then be a considerable jump in performance required before the worker can earn more than the allowance
and he may decline ever to make the attempt.

Whatever the method of making an interim payment might be, it
must be recognized as a cost against the productivity agreement and the
eventual payments due on full implementation must be tailored to
ensure that the interim cost is recovered. In other words, an interim
award should be regarded as an advance of wages against predictable
productivity benefits.

THE ROLE OF SUPERVISION

On the shoulders of front-line supervision now rests the success of
the whole operation. All the hard thinking, preparation and negotiation
will be wasted effort if the provisions of the productivity agreement are
not applied conscientiously in every department, to each individual.

Line management and supervision will have had training in the
philosophy of productivity bargaining generally and in their own
company's approach in particular. They will have been kept in touch
with the progress of the deal and, on the signing of the agreement.
the manner in which their own salaries can be improved will be
confirmed, either individually or, if there is a staff union, by formal
agreement with the union.

Now they must be acquainted thoroughly with the way in which the
provisions of the productivity agreement will be applied. It is suggested
that, in addition to general meetings, there should be meetings of each
department's supervisors immediately preceding, and coincident with,
the implementation of the agreement to that department. There will thus
be an opportunity for the detailed explanation and examination of the
supervisor's role apropos his individual working situation. Unless this
is done there is a very real danger that the full benefits of the agreement will never be realized. If from the beginning the supervisor does
not insist on provisions such as flexibility or adherence to starting
and finishing times, it is probable that these provisions will never be
applied as they were intended and agreed.

THE ROLE OF TOP MANAGEMENT

The implementation stage is the dangerous age for a productivity
deal. All of the dramatic work—the preparation, announcing the
proposals, signing the agreement—has been done, and there is a temptation to assume that everything will now start to happen of its own

accord. Nowhere is this danger greater than at the top management level, and if the Board slackens its efforts at this stage, it is inevitable that momentum will be slowed and opportunities lost further down the line.

There is a particular danger of this if there have been significant top management changes since the productivity bargaining process started. It might be difficult for a newcomer to comprehend the pressures and policies leading up to the bargain. At the very least the newcomer —unless he is unusually perceptive—will not be enthusiastic and it is continued enthusiasm and interest from all members of the Board that is needed as much at the implementation stage as at any other stage of the bargain. There can be no relaxation of this energy and interest at the top until the bargain is part of the everyday life of the company.

SETTING UP A FORMAL COMMUNICATIONS STRUCTURE

If the agreement provides for the establishment or revision of a formal employee/management communications structure, this should be set up at the earliest possible stage. The aim should be to emphasize communication at the departmental level but there will be matters which have a plant-wide interest. The system must therefore include a central consultative committee. The advisability of ensuring that employees' representatives on formal consultative committees are accredited shop stewards has already been mentioned in the section on preparing the communications network. The question of supervisory representation on joint consultative committees is often raised. This is usually prompted less by a desire by the supervisors to have a formal channel of communication with more senior management than by a desire to know what communications pass between more senior management and shop floor representatives. So often, joint consultative procedures leave the supervisor in the dark—unless he cares to ask the shop steward. To a large extent this is overcome by the use of departmental committees, at which the supervisor is part of the management representation. To meet the problem of the central committee it is suggested that a meeting of supervisors is held immediately after the main committee meeting to give them a summary of the proceedings. It is also recommended that one or more non-supervisory staff representatives—depending on the size and the unionization of staff—should sit on the central committee. Much of the matter discussed will be of no direct interest to them, but the increasing coincidence of works and staff conditions and procedures will lead to more and more common interest subjects. The increasing interest of staff in productivity bargaining and the need to consider them in comprehensive bargaining is mentioned later.

An example of the constitution of a formal communications structure is given at Appendix 5.

INFORMATION DISPLAY

Once a start has been made on implementing a productivity agreement, one problem is to maintain impetus and interest. This involves deliberate thought and attention to giving adequate publicity to everything affecting the agreement. This will include such things as the company results, forward load and sales as well as more immediately relevant information on performances, bonus earned and so on.

Large display boards are required in each department, positioned so that everyone can see them and has to pass by them. Various charting techniques can be used—graphs are not always well understood, thermometers are easier to appreciate. Colour is essential. News items should be changed frequently—displays of new products, photographs of end uses, exhibitions showing the cost of tools and consumables—these can all generate interest in added value and the company as a whole.

Sometimes a weekly or monthly news letter proves to be a useful stimulus. It must be short and tabloid with photographs, humour and an emphasis on success and achievement.

Management at all levels needs this sort of information just as much as the workers. High productivity is often largely a question of morale and confidence and this has to be engendered everywhere.

If this information job is to be done properly, someone has to be made responsible for it. It requires someone who is enthusiastic about the productivity agreement as well as being an enthusiast by nature, with a flair for visual publicity.

This aspect is frequently overlooked by management because they are not always reliable judges of what appeals to their employees. The management may not read the daily tabloids or watch commercial television but their workers do. A good guide to the tastes of the worker is to be found in the communication media they buy and watch.

SECTIONAL PRODUCTIVITY BARGAINS

As its name suggests, a sectional bargain (sometimes called a 'partial' or 'local' bargain) is one which is concerned with only part of a plant. Sectional bargains do not often make the headlines but there are very many more of them than comprehensive bargains. They are thus an important part of industrial life and merit more generous consideration than they have had. The relatively little comment on sectional productivity bargaining has tended to be critical, largely, one suspects, because the disadvantages are so obvious. Chief among them is the comparatively superficial nature of sectional agreements; because they deal with only part of the work force it is unlikely that fundamental changes can be attempted, and the change in attitudes so often generated by a comprehensive agreement is seldom found in sectional deals. Other disadvantages include the distortion of the wage structure by a sectional wage increase, resulting either in an increase of leap-frogging claims or in conflicting priority demands for subsequent sectional deals. It is also inevitable that some departments will offer more scope for productivity improvement than others and there could therefore be variations in the resulting increases.

It is suggested that most of these problems can be overcome by developing a company strategy for sectional bargaining. This should be discussed with the senior shop stewards, the local officials and the D.E.P. etc., in much the same way as the comprehensive bargain. One of the provisions of the company policy should be that whilst only one section might be directly concerned in the productivity improvement, the resulting benefits should be shared throughout the plant. If the amount on the hourly rate would be ludicrously small, it could be given in a lump sum as an annual holiday or Christmas bonus. Shop stewards and local officials are likely to see the merit of this because it maintains the wage differentials and does not present them with the problems of a privileged group in the factory. They will also recognize that, although only one sectional deal might be immediately anticipated, others are bound to follow and work people throughout the company will enjoy a steady rise in wage rates.

The pressures on management resources and top management time are considerably reduced by sectional bargaining, the need for consultants' help will be considerably lessened and possibly eliminated altogether. The steps described for a comprehensive bargain—assessing the gains and costs, formulating the proposals, preparing the ground, D.E.P. approval and negotiating and implementing the agreement—must all be covered for the sectional bargain, but the number of people involved is reduced and the time needed for each stage is less. It must be recognized however that the total effort and time is not proportionally less than for the comprehensive agreement, and in the long-term a series of sectional agreements will represent a greater total burden than the single plant-wide agreement. On the communications side, for instance, everyone in the plant must know what is happening with each successive sectional deal and must know how it affects them in the short-term and the long-term. The total communications effort therefore is more complex and of greater duration.

Comprehensive productivity bargaining must always be the first choice, if only because it is more likely to achieve fundamental changes. Sectional productivity bargaining will rightfully commend itself to those companies where, for one reason or another, a comprehensive deal is out of the question.

REDUNDANCY

A number of the early, well-reported, productivity bargains were based on a substantial reduction of manning and, perhaps because of this, the association of productivity bargaining and redundancy has been given undue emphasis. In fact very few productivity bargains result in redundancy. Almost all of them will include provision for reduced man-hours but this will normally be achieved by curtailing overtime and, if necessary, reducing manning by normal wastage. A company can anticipate its productivity bargain a considerable time ahead. This, coupled with the length of the period of implementation, will afford it every opportunity to take advantage of its normal turnover rate, so that people are not replaced, or are replaced only on a temporary basis.

In spite of this, there will be occasions when a company has no practical alternative to redundancy as a means of increasing its productivity. If this is so, it will be foreseen in the planning stage and must be clearly explained in the proposals. If a redundancy policy exists, it might be used for dealing with the productivity agreement redundancies. It is likely, however, that the policy was framed with the thought of a forced reduction resulting from economic difficulties rather than a planned reduction to improve the prosperity of the company and its terms will probably be capable of considerable improvement. A company can afford to be reasonably generous in such a situation. The precise terms are a matter for discussion and decision within the company and will be influenced considerably by employment prospects in the area. It is recommended that, all other things being equal, the scheme is weighted heavily in favour of the older employee who might find it more difficult to find, and settle in, other employment. Obviously a company will use all of its resources to find redundant employees work in the area. The local employment exchanges should be given plenty of warning in addition to that required to qualify for Redundancy Payments Act rebates. Redundancies caused by productivity bargaining can be dealt with over such a long period that it is most unlikely that any extreme difficulties or hardship will be encountered.

Even if no redundancy is foreseen it is advisable, as mentioned earlier, to take the opportunity of the productivity proposals to devise a redundancy policy if none is in existence.

HOW LONG?

It is impossible without knowing the company involved to give more than a general indication of the length of time that should be allowed for productivity bargaining. So much depends on the particular situation of the company—its specialist resources, the effectiveness of its wage structure, the accuracy of its work measurement and the state of its industrial relations. For the average company—if there is such a thing—employing about five hundred people, with good specialist resources supplemented by consultants, the following timetable would not be exceptional.

Investigations to establish the feasibility of a deal, activity sampling, devising productivity indices, work measurement, job evaluation and incentive schemes .. .. 26 weeks
Preparation of proposals, training of managers, supervisors, shop stewards .. .. 8 weeks
Negotiation .. .. 10 weeks
Implementation .. .. 20 weeks

A sectional bargain for say fifty people might be accomplished in three months.

STAFF WORKERS AND PRODUCTIVITY BARGAINING

A comprehensive productivity bargain is commonly comprehensive only in the sense that it covers all manual workers in a company, any effects on staff being limited to protecting supervisors' differentials. The practice of excluding staff from productivity bargains is understandable. The areas of greatest contribution—and of greatest pressure for wage increases—are usually to be found on the shop floor. There are obvious problems in including staff in an over-all agreement: attitudes and orientation are different, unionisation is non-existent or weaker, negotiating practices and procedure differ. These, however, are arguments for a separate agreement for the staff worker rather than for his exclusion.

The productivity benefits of a staff agreement, although not as great as those from the shop floor, are by no means insignificant. Methods of measurement for staff workers, such as those mentioned in Chapter 2, have led to reductions of 30 per cent and more in staff numbers.

When formulating proposals for a shop floor agreement, therefore, the preparation of separate proposals for staff workers should be considered. In all essentials—job evaluation, payment structure, preparations, etc.,—the pattern is the same as that for manual workers.

8

Monitoring, Reviewing and Developing the Productivity Agreement

As the various facets of the productivity agreement are implemented, it is necessary to install systems to record results and to make comparisons with the original plans. This has to be done on a continuous monitoring basis and also in more comprehensive fashion, from time to time. From both of these feed backs, information will be obtained which will indicate both shortcomings and opportunities in the agreement. This, together with knowledge of the future plans of the company and its man-power and industrial relations strategy, will enable the productivity agreement to be developed.

MONITORING

The monitoring aspect is largely concerned with information on productivity, wages, value added etc. so that expenditure and benefits can be assessed. It is also essential to monitor the detailed changes in the agreement as time goes on.

MONITORING RESULTS

The measurement of work, productivity and added values depends on information provided from the shop floor or the office floor or its equivalent. The value of accurate work measurement or statistically validated analysis of productivity will be lost by incorrect reporting of information. Where incentives are involved, there is a pressure to falsify information in order to generate a superiously high performance and hence bonus. It is not only the worker who may be tempted to report more work than has been done. Management at all levels, under pressure from a particular worker group, may slacken standards and add allowances which are not justified by the facts, thus inflating earnings and bringing a short respite.

It is therefore essential to get across to management and particularly foremen and supervisors, the importance of accurate booking of information. Unless the highest possible standards are set, the whole productivity agreement is liable to drift towards eventual ineffectiveness. The danger of linking the pay of a supervisor directly with that of his workers is evident.

As to the workers, it is hoped that they will play fair by the agreement and there is no doubt that the vast majority generally will. However, it is unrealistic to expect the highest standards if management is slack about surveillance. Checks on the accuracy of booking must therefore be made regularly, if not continuously, and the fact that this is being done should be made evident to all. It is often possible to fit measuring instruments, such as counters and recorders of electricity consumption, to machines. A reconciliation of work recorded with production control information of batch quantity and parts scrapped is an essential check. This is facilitated by shop floor data-logging equipment used in conjunction with computerized production control systems. If really water-tight arrangements can be made, it is unnecessary to emphasize penalties for false booking. The actual imposition of penalties often does more harm than good but the existence of a penalty will be an effective jog to the conscience.

Some of the important information which should be monitored is listed below:

I   DIRECT WORKERS—INDIVIDUAL AND SMALL GROUPS—WORK
    MEASUREMENT
    For each individual or small group as appropriate:

$$\text{performance in terms of} \frac{\text{standard minutes}}{\text{clock minutes}} \times 100 \text{ per cent}$$

        on productive work.
    lost time in categories related to responsibility,
    analysis of standard minutes produced into productive work,
    unmeasured work, experimental work and approved non-
    productive work,
    from the above can be assessed the number of SMs produced
    per clock hour,
    gross wage per hour,
    gross cost per Standard Minute,
    machine hours per week,
    machine availability (per cent),
    overtime hours per week,
    physical measures of output per machine hour—by machine
    where appropriate.

II   INDIRECT WORKERS
    For each department and overall, for each week
        numbers and hours

$$\text{rates of} \frac{\text{indirect hours}}{\text{direct hours}}$$

        overtime hours
        individual or group performances if labour planning and
        control techniques are in use.

III   ALL WORKERS—LARGE GROUPS—PRODUCTIVITY MEASUREMENT
For each department and overall, for each week or month
   input hours,
   output,
   change in work in progress,
   values of any important variables which it is agreed affects
   the measurement of productivity.

IV   ALL WORKERS—ADDED VALUE
Overall for each period
   sales (£)
   materials (£)
   consumables (£)
   bought out services (£)
   sales value of changes in work in progress and finished
   stocks (£)
   added value (£)
   labour cost (£)
   $$\frac{\text{labour cost}}{\text{added value}}$$
   base period labour cost based in historical ratio (£)
   bonus available (£)

V   INDICATORS OF WORKERS' ATTITUDES
For each department and overall
   absenteeism
   labour turnover
   labour retention
   timekeeping

MONITORING THE DETAILED CHANGES IN THE AGREEMENT
The documents comprising the productivity bargain will lay down
a number of rules which will govern its operation. However, as soon
as a start is made in implementation, a succession of detailed settlements
on interpretation will be set in motion. Unforeseen events will occur
which will require ad hoc remedies.

Every detailed agreement modifies the initial bargain and becomes
the basis on which further negotiations are conducted.

It is essential therefore that every agreement or arrangement, however trivial, is accurately documented. It is best that this is done
formally—for example, on a specially designed form, copies of which
are given to the workers' representatives. These forms should be filed
together and an adequate index maintained.

Care should be taken to distinguish between isolated cases and
cases which set a precedent. The anomalies of industrial life are so
numerous that concessions are justified in particular cases. Management
are often reluctant to make such concessions for fear that they establish
precedents which will become the basis for a wider range of claims.

If agreement can be reached and documented, as each case is settled, on whether it constitutes a precedent or not, then the benefits of increased flexibility in negotiating will have been gained. The formalization that is advocated involves persuading all concerned in negotiations to write up the agreements reached on the standard form and to have this numbered, filed and indexed. If this is not done, details of agreements will appear in a variety of forms, memos, letters, notes, etc., and in a variety of places. Invariably some will be lost or overlooked. This leads to confusion and doubts and in due course to a breakdown of confidence.

ASSESSMENT OF BENEFITS, ANNUAL REVIEW

For each component part of the bargain, there should be a statement of the before-the-bargain situation and costs, and a forecast of the situation and costs expected after implementation.

Reference has already been made to the monitoring of results. It is not practicable to monitor everything or to assess the total position continuously. Provision should therefore be made for a periodic audit and a period of one year between audits is a convenient and practical interval.

The carrying out of this periodic audit should be envisaged from the outset. Hence an early involvement of the accounting function is vital whilst the productivity bargain is being developed. A productivity bargain has already been likened to a capital investment. The success of the investment will depend on its capital cost, operating cost, useful life and on the benefits obtained, which may depend on important marketing assumptions such as market share and selling prices. These are all vital before-and-after quantifications of the bargain.

There will be other benefits envisaged such as reduction of labour turnover, ability to recruit scarce skills, simplification of the administration of the wages system, control of wages drift, stability of earnings, flexibility and mobility of labour, etc.

The periodic audit may be considered as a management review, or may be established, as part of the bargain, as a basis for review by the signatories to the bargain. If the bargain is to be the start of a continuous dialogue between the workers and management over a number of years, then there is much to be said for a frank and open annual review in which the workers' representatives are fully involved.

THE PRODUCTIVITY AGREEMENT—MANPOWER AND INDUSTRIAL RELATIONS STRATEGY

The productivity agreement may be seen as the beginning of a process of identifying the worker increasingly with the firm. If the agreement genuinely relates productivity and pay, then the worker will be given more information about factors affecting productivity and hence about the way the firm is managed. The communication channels which are developed for this purpose can lead to a greater understanding and

H

agreement about the problems and aspirations of both workers and company. This in turn can lead to improved relationships.

None of this will be of much use unless the company is clear where it is going both in terms of its future manpower requirements and its industrial relation policies.

The corporate long range plan of a company should indicate the quantities, location and type of labour that will be required over a period of 5–10 years. The probable availability of labour will be a factor that will have been considered in drawing up the corporate plans. Generally, the company will be in competition with a variety of alternative employers. As housing and transport become less and less a limitation on mobility, workers will move to more congenial employment. All other things being equal, there will be an attraction to areas with a better climate and with better amenities. The working conditions, management policies and remuneration in any given firm will require to be such as to attract the required number and quality of workers. If the firm is in an area where climate and amenities are poor, it will have to provide more attractive working conditions than one in a high amenity area.

The productivity agreement is central to this situation for it should reflect a company's thinking on attracting and holding workers and in motivating them to give of their best. The future development of the agreement equally should reflect the company's thinking on these aspects and on the means of achieving them in the light of expected future changes.

The topics that require consideration and forecasting include:

the changing nature of the jobs that workers will be required to do,
the types of job that workers will be willing to do in the future,
changes in the mix of contributions required of the workers,
changes in the benefits workers will expect from the company.

The long-term trend may well emphasize less the satisfaction of material needs and more the psychological needs. With the elimination of the dissatisfiers of poor working conditions, low pay etc. taken for granted, the need will be to give greater scope for job enlargement, responsibility, recognition and promotion.

The worker can also be expected to become more interested in the growth prospects of the firm for which he works and in the efficiency and effectiveness of the management.

It would be a doctrine of perfection to suggest that all these future aspects should be foreseen before concluding a productivity agreement. However, it is essential to try to predict changes that might affect the agreement in the next five years or so. A more important point is to realize the need for changing and for modifying the agreement as time goes on. This implies a need to understand fully all the factors affecting manpower requirements and industrial relations strategy. The productivity agreement is therefore only a beginning.

Appendix 1

Examples of Productivity Agreement Proposals

EXAMPLE 1

TUBES LIMITED, BIRMINGHAM

SUMMARY OF PROPOSALS

The proposals include:
- (a) A completely new and simplified wages system.
- (b) Changes in working methods and practices.
- (c) Changes in employment standards.
- (d) Proposals for full Joint Consultation.
- (e) A detailed Security of Employment plan.

THE WAGES SYSTEM

Wage rates will increase on average by 19 per cent. The improved efficiency resulting from the agreement is expected to raise productivity by 25 per cent.

The main elements of the simplified structure are these.

1. *A high basic rate*

Five grades have been established by Job Evaluation and each grade has a separate basic rate. This rate amounts to 75 per cent of the earnings of a direct worker working at standard rate. For employees whose work is not directly measured the basic rate will be 80 per cent of earnings at standard rate.

Each Job Grade will also have a time rate which will move in relation to the Engineering Industry National Agreement, and which will be used for the calculation of overtime, holiday pay, shift allowances, etc.

2. *Individual Bonus*

To be paid to all employees whose work, either as an individual or as a member of a gang or small group, can be accurately measured. Performance is to be measured by the most appropriate work measurement techniques. It is anticipated on average that these employees will be able to earn 20 per cent of their basic rate under this part of the wages scheme. However, the average amount of money will vary according to the grade of the employee.

H*

3. *Departmental Productivity Bonus*

This bonus will be paid to every employee in the works. It will reward the co-operation, flexibility and willingness of employees. It will be measured by the productivity of the main areas of the works. At a 100 per cent performance the amount of this incentive bonus will be 13½ per cent of Basic Rate for those covered by the Direct Incentive and 20 per cent of Basic Rate for Indirect Workers.

4. *Annual Improvement Factor*

Increases in added value relative to wages costs will be reflected in increases in all basic rates.

STABILITY OF EARNINGS

Increased stability is fundamentally achieved by the high basic rate which will be used for the payment of all attendance hours even if work is not available. Stability is further improved by two other proposals. First, employees' performance under the incentive parts of the wages system will be averaged—monthly averages will be used in the case of direct bonuses and a three-monthly average in the case of departmental bonus. The average performance for one monthly period will establish the level of pay for the next month. Secondly, the direct and indirect incentive bonuses will be paid in increments related to bands of performance. Against each band an amount of bonus will be paid according to which grade the employee's job is in. The higher the band the higher the bonus. The bands are quite wide so that small variations in performance will not alter the amount of money paid. Operators will be warned if their performance drops to the lower level of their band.

SHIFT ALLOWANCES

Allowances for two and three eight-hour shift working will be well in excess of those nationally agreed. Similar payments will be used for continuous shift working in the Maintenance Departments coupled with an additional Disturbance Allowance.

TRAINING ALLOWANCE

Trainees will have their own set of basic rates and a new method of payment has been devised which will be used for calculation of the 'Individual Bonus' for the payment of Trainee Direct Workers.

SUB-STANDARD WORK

All payment for hours spent on producing work not of the required standard and within the operator's control will be deducted from earnings at the earliest opportunity following detection of the faulty work.

ALLOWANCES

Cash allowances over and above the grade rates will be restricted to a Hot Worker's Allowance paid to employees who, for more than 75 per cent of their shift, work within 10 feet of an open furnace or workpiece at a temperature in excess of 1,000°C. and are exposed to radiant heat.

WAITING TIME

Periods of time beyond employees' control, when they are unable to continue on productive work will be paid at their basic rate plus the department productivity bonus.

TRANSFERS

Where a worker is temporarily transferred to another job, he will be paid in the same way as he would have been on his normal job.

Where a man is permanently transferred to a new job in a lower job grade there will be a transitional phase from one grade to the next of three months. During this three months his Basic Rate will be decreased by one-third of the difference between the Job Grade Rates. The worker will be credited with any Training Allowances to which he is entitled.

PROTECTION OF EARNINGS AWARDS

Prior to the introduction of the new wage structure into a department the average hourly earnings of all operatives who are to remain on the same job under the new wage arrangements will be calculated for three months prior to the introduction of the scheme. This will be compared with the anticipated hourly earnings at standard performance under the new Individual Bonus plus the Departmental Bonus plus the Basic Rate. Premium time will not be included in the calculations.

It is anticipated that in a small number of cases the previous average hourly earnings will be in excess of the revised earnings. Where this is so a supplementary hourly rate, called a 'Protection of Earnings Award (PEA)', will be paid to the worker in addition to his earnings under the new wages structure. This PEA will be equivalent to the difference between the old and new earnings level.

Any increase in the basic rate resulting from plant negotiations or prompted by a National award will be deducted from the PEA. This will also be the case where the Basic Rate is increased by the operation of the 'Annual Improvement Factor' provisions.

Should a man permanently change his job after the implementation of the new wage structure the PEA will immediately cease. Furthermore, PEA will only be paid to those workers who have been on the job in question for a period of three months or more prior to the introduction of the new wage structure to their job.

CHANGES IN WORKING METHODS AND PRACTICES AND IN EMPLOYMENT STANDARDS

It is in the interests of employees and the company to ensure the most efficient use of labour, material and machinery so that competitive efficiency is continually being improved. Sales forecasts for the next few years suggest that not all of the increased productivity possible can be absorbed by increased sales. Some increase in productivity must therefore be achieved by a reduction in man-hours. The proposals in this section are designed to do this and to establish the work on a basis from which it can respond effectively to sales requirements. They include changes in:
1. Hours of work.
2. Job Enlargement and Flexibility of Labour.
3. Employment Standards and conditions, e.g. absenteeism, time-keeping, tea breaks.

HOURS OF WORK

Systematic overtime is to be abolished, and additional overtime will be authorized only to meet emergencies on a short-term basis. It is a declared intention of the agreement to cut down the long hours many employees have been asked to work in recent years. The new rates of pay are designed to give a competitive level of earnings for a basic week and monetary pressures for employees to work overtime should therefore be reduced.

It is also proposed to increase the amount of shift working and to simplify the shift systems which are worked in the factory. The following shift systems will be those primarily used:
(a) Double-Dayshift.
(b) Rotating three shifts.
(c) Rotating four shifts (probably confined to Maintenance Departments).

The normal dayshift will also feature in the shift systems, but the permanent nightshift will be replaced by other systems.

The company reserves the right to determine the optimum shift pattern for each department and to change the pattern for individuals or departments where changing requirements make this necessary. Changes for departments will always be preceded by consultation. Flexibility of the shift pattern will help to increase departmental productivity bonuses and the Annual Improvement Factor.

JOB ENLARGEMENT AND FLEXIBILITY OF LABOUR

The simplified five grade structure and higher basic and fall back rates will permit increased flexibility and mobility of labour. In particular, an examination will be made by each department of the jobs which fall within a grade. Wherever possible an employee will be trained in more than one job in his grade, and occasionally in other grades (usually in the employee's department). This will make the best use of the employee's time, experience and ability and reduce the number of occasions on which employees are transferred to work on lower grades. Payment of the new rates is conditional upon employees agreeing to undertake the training necessary and carry out the increased variety of work. Examples of improved flexibility sought are:

Maintenance and services personnel will carry out tasks which they have the knowledge and the tools to do satisfactorily, as and when the occasion arises.

Employees are prepared to transfer to other work (outside that covered by the Job Enlargement programme) when this is necessary. Payment levels in such cases will in no event be less that the fall-back rate.

EMPLOYMENT STANDARDS AND CONDITIONS

(a) *Basic Principles*

The company disciplinary policies are based on the following principles:

Each supervisor is accountable for the conduct and discipline of his subordinates.

Employees are expected to behave within the law of the land, the company rules, and in accordance with codes of behaviour generally accepted within a community.

Respect for the company's property, whether buildings, machinery, materials or tools, is taken as obvious, as is respect for the person and property of other employees.

(b) *Time-keeping and Absenteeism*

The proposals make detailed provision for establishing fair and uniform standards to be observed concerning time-keeping and absenteeism, and lay down penalties for non-observance of these standards.

(c) *Tea Breaks*

The company proposes to abolish all regular tea breaks and to introduce vending machines so that employees can take refreshment as opportunities in the course of their work present themselves.

(d) *Breaches of Discipline and Appeals Procedure*

A set procedure is laid down in the event of a breach of discipline and also in the case of an appeal. A special procedure has also been set up to deal with appeals against Work Study standards.

COMMUNICATIONS STRUCTURE

The communications structure will be improved and will have two main aims:

to inform employees about managerial practices, policies, attitudes and objectives.

to feed back to management the effects of these together with employee reactions and suggestions for improvement.

The new structure will have three components.

1. COMMAND STRUCTURE

The command structure is the executive chain of command and should be used as the means whereby work is authorized, controlled and accounted for. This structure is the predominant channel of communication, and employees' problems should always be referred initially to their immediate supervisor.

2. NEGOTIATING STRUCTURE

The negotiating committee will be the body which deals basically with pay and working conditions.

It is proposed that a small Negotiating Committee be established, comprising six members. Management representatives would be the Production Manager, Personnel Manager, and the Chief Industrial Engineer. Employee representatives would be the Senior Shop Steward of the T.G.W.U., and the A.E.U. and the E.T.U. Shop Stewards. This Negotiating Committee would meet regularly to discuss and resolve matters arising from the implementation of the agreement, and after implementation it would meet as and when necessary.

3. ADVISORY STRUCTURE

The advisory structure will consist of an integrated two-tier consultative system of a works advisory council, and departmental productivity panels. The principal aims are:

to keep employees informed of the company's trading position.

to use the knowledge and experience of employees' representatives to test the validity of proposed changes in policies, machines, systems, etc.

to provide the opportunity for employees to comment on all aspects of the company's business and to make formal suggestions for its improvement.

DEPARTMENTAL PRODUCTIVITY PANELS

There will be five departmental productivity panels covering the factory, in which employee representatives will join management and supervision in considering means of increasing productivity. These panels will discuss all matters related to increased productivity in the department and will review the progress of the indirect incentive. The panels will provide an opportunity for employees to comment on and contribute to the department's productive efficiency, and make suggestions for improvement. The panels are not empowered to discuss any matters which are directly covered by T.U. agreements.

The composition and constitution of these panels will be decided after consultation with employee representatives.

WORKS ADVISORY COUNCIL

Each departmental productivity panel will elect two members to serve on the Works Advisory Council, which will be the co-ordinating body of the Advisory Structure. It will review the progress of the Works overall, discuss all important matters referred to it by the productivity Panels, and consider the Works performance in relation to the Annual Improvement Factor. Membership of the Council will consist of an ex officio Chairman—the Works Director, Management representatives, Union representatives, and the five elected representatives of the Departmental panels. Two joint secretaries will be appointed. One will be ex officio, the Personnel Manager—the other will be elected from employees' representatives. The Chairman may appoint sub-committees to report back to the Council on specific matters. As for meetings—they will be held every month, though extraordinary meetings may be held to meet emergencies.

SECURITY OF EMPLOYMENT PLAN

The Company recognizes that security of employment is one of the primary needs of working life. It has therefore included in the Productivity Agreement a carefully designed plan, which ensures that redundancy will only occur as a last resort, after all measures to prevent it have been fully explored.

Measures to avoid redundancy:
1. Curtail recruitment.
2. Transfers, which will include re-training where necessary.
3. Reduction of overtime.
4. Short-time working for a limited period.

Dismissal Criteria (should above measures fail)

When employees are to be declared redundant, their selection shall take place in the following order.

Male Employees over the age of 65; female employees over 60.

Volunteers.

Short service employees in preference to long service employees.

The plan provides for additional warning to be given to that established by law and sets up an Appeals Committee to consider the case of any employee who feels that he has been unfairly treated.

Other Points

Efforts will be made by the Company to help redundant employees obtain alternative employment.

An employee who has been declared redundant by the Company shall have preferential consideration over other applicants for re-employment by the Company.

Finally, the Company will keep the appropriate employees' representatives fully informed from the moment that the probability of redundancy is foreseen.

INTERIM AWARD

An additional hourly payment will be made to employees from the date the proposals are accepted until the changes proposed have been made and the new rates paid. The interim payment is conditional upon full co-operation in the implementation of the proposals and on increases in productivity in the factory of 6 per cent after three months and 9 per cent after ten months.

EXAMPLE 2

PARKINSON COWAN APPLIANCES LTD.

In addition to a number of proposals already covered by the Tubes Limited example, the Parkinson Cowan Appliances agreement contained a number of novel ideas, among which were the following.

JOB EVALUATION PROCEDURE

Instead of undertaking job evaluation as a combined management/union exercise, the company asked a committee of shop stewards to evaluate all jobs in the factory and grade them. The stewards concerned were allowed to use their full time on the evaluation and produced the results in four weeks. With the exception of one or two minor changes, the evaluation was totally acceptable to management.

CHANGES IN JOB VALUES

The agreement overcomes the common problem of changing incorrect job values by the following procedure:

Standard Performance for a job is introduced for a period of four months.

At the end of the above period either the Management or the Trade Union members may appeal against the Standard Performance.

Where mutually revised Standard Values increase or decrease an employees earnings, a sum is payable and calculated on eight weeks of the differences of the old level and revised level of earnings.

Following this exercise, the Standard Values are mutually accepted by Management and the Trade Unions for a period of twelve months, at the end of which either side may ask for a review of the Standard Values. The aim and purpose of this review is to maintain an acceptable level of earnings for similar effort on similar tasks and avoid a large spread of earnings throughout the works.

Those values which realize a level of earnings outside of the tolerances are readjusted. When the level of earnings is reduced, compensation paid is based on sixteen weeks payment of the differential between the existing and revised bonus earnings for forty hours.

Where there is evidence that an individual has failed to maintain the agreed standard of performance, the case is investigated jointly by the Management and the Trade Unions.

In the event of disagreement on Standard Values, a Committee of three members of Management and three Shop Stewards endeavours to settle the matter.

INTRODUCTION OF NEW VALUES

Employees earning below the new standard values are increased immediately. Those earning more than the new value established for their jobs are given the option of retaining their existing level of earnings or accepting a 'buy-out' of their differential based on the following formula:

1. Immediate buy out   —   12 months' differential
2. After 6 months   —   9 months' differential
3. After 12 months   —   6 months' differential
4. After 18 months   —   3 months' differential

Those who opt to retain their present level accept that they will get no increase until, by annual Added Value additions or National Awards, the assessed standard value overtakes their current level.

EQUAL PAY

Female operatives' rates are equivalent to the lowest manual grade.

IDENTIFYING PRODUCTIVITY IMPROVEMENT

In addition to a standard commitment to accept improved methods and machines, etc., every section of the factory is studied jointly by management and trade unions to establish ways of improving efficiency.

Appendix 2

Profile of Contributions to Productivity

1. Direct production workers have a very important contribution to make to small group productivity which is not at present being made. There is already good attention to quality and material utilization. Direct labour also has an important contribution to make to Departmental productivity, machine productivity and delivery performance. This pattern continues through in the wider consideration of the firm and take in the potential for improvements in the use of consumables.

2. The indirect production workers in this Company do not appear to have the potential to make an important contribution.

3. The maintenance and craft workers have a good way to go in increasing their contributions towards small group productivity. They also have plenty to contribute towards departmental productivity.

4. The clerical workers could improve their contribution towards delivery performance (for example, by improving production control activities).

5. Supervision and management appear to be operating reasonably well in their fields but middle management may well be under-estimating their potential contributions towards improving small group and departmental productivity.

This form indicates the view of the assessor about the importance of contributions that can be made. This provides some information about the assessor himself. Several assessments will provide information about areas of disagreement between assessors. The same observations apply to the assessment of the present position.

The form is about contributions to the production areas of the firm. It does not therefore give a complete picture of the clerical, supervision and middle-management contributions. The form has spaces for some of these other contributions.

COMPANY...

| PROFILE OF CONTRIBUTIONS |

SCORING: 1 – INSIGNIFICANT, 2 – SIGNIFICANT,

MARK ▷ – PRESENT POSITION

ASSESSOR...

Type of Contribution / Category of Worker	Higher Output of Machine or Small Group			Higher Labour Productivity of Department				
	Individual Performance	Machine or Small Group - Output/Hour	Quality of Output	Labour Productivity	Material Productivity	Machine Productivity	Output	Delivery Performance
DIRECT PRODUCTION	2/5	2/5	4/5	2/4	2/2	2/5	1/1	1/3
INDIRECT PRODUCTION	1/2	1/2	1/1	1/2	1/1	1/2	1/2	1/1
MAINTENANCE & CRAFT	2/4	2/5	2/5	2/4	1/2	2/4	1/2	2/3
CLERICAL	2/2	N/A	2/2	1/1	1/1	1/1	1/1	2/4
SUPERVISION	3/4	3/4	3/4	2/3	2/2	2/3	3/4	3/3
MIDDLE-MANAGEMENT	2/2	2/2	2/3	2/2	2/3	2/2	2/3	2/3

APPENDIX 2

Fig. 16

DEPARTMENT...

T O   P R O D U C T I V I T Y

3 – FAIRLY IMPORTANT, 4 – IMPORTANT, 5 – VERY IMPORTANT

△B – POTENTIAL POSITION

DATE..

	Greater Prosperity Opportunities of the Firm										
Labour Productivity	Material Productivity	Machine Productivity	Consumables Productivity	Output	Delivery Performance						
1 / 2	1 / 1	1 / 3	1 / 3	1 / 3	2 / 3						
1 / 2	1 / 1	1 / 2	1 / 2	1 / 2	1 / 1						
1 / 2	1 / 1	2 / 3	1 / 3	1 / 3	2 / 3						
1 / 1	1 / 1	1 / 1	1 / 1	1 / 1	2 / 4						
2 / 2	2 / 2	2 / 3	2 / 3	3 / 3	3 / 3						
4 / 5	3 / 4	4 / 5	2 / 3	4 / 5	4 / 5						

Appendix 3

Management Surveys

Management surveys in connection with productivity bargaining are usually directed at departmental managers and foremen. The approach is broadly similar to that used for the employee attitude survey, but questions can be more pointed (except where the morale of the supervision itself might be covered) and because of the smaller numbers, all the people concerned can be approached instead of restricting to a sample.

A simple indication of the style and questions is given below.

MANAGEMENT SURVEY

There are no 'tricks' in this form and there is no need to ponder on any question. Just put a tick against the statement you know or think is true. If you have no knowledge of the question just leave it blank.

Are you a manager?

       a supervisor?

Is the labour you control mainly skilled?

                     unskilled?

                     male?

                     female?

The following are common obstacles to effciency. How much do they affect Grasp and Grind Ltd.?

	A lot	Not too much	A little
Timekeeping: clocking on late.	——	——	——
Starting late on the job and finishing early.	——	——	——
Absenteeism.	——	——	——
Difficulties of moving people to different shifts.	——	——	——

Etcetera . . .

Most employees leave because of earnings

                              working conditions

                              shift work

                              lack of prospects

                              insecurity.

What proportion of non-skilled shop floor workers in your department is in a union?

                              About 100 per cent.

                              Over half.

                              Less than half.

                              Very few.

How many shop stewards have the full confidence of their members?

                              All of them.

                              Most.

                              Very few.

Do you get good advice and help on

	Yes	No	Not my concern
(a) dealing with union claims?	——	——	——
(b) dealing with disciplinary matters?	——	——	——

Etcetera . . .

Appendix 4

Attitude Surveys

Attitude surveys used in connection with productivity bargaining seek to obtain an indication of the morale of the employees concerned, their ideas for improvements in employment conditions and the effectiveness of their work, and the probably response to particular types of change and to change in general. Surveys are usually undertaken on a representative sample by the use of a questionnaire and follow-up interviews. It follows that questionnaires should be specially designed for each application and should preferably be administered by consultants or some other body distinct from the management.

A simple example of the style and questions is given below.

QUESTIONNAIRE

This questionnaire has been designed to give us the views on various matters of employees of Grasp and Grind Limited. We should be grateful if you would quickly read through the form, putting a tick against the words which most closely express your answer. If you do not feel you can answer a particular question just leave it blank. The answers are confidential and in any case you will see that you do not need to give your identity. An addressed envelope is attached for the return of the questionnaire to us.

1. Is your work   skilled?
                               unskilled?
                               semi-skilled?

2. Are you   a day worker?
                               a shift worker?
                               paid a variable bonus?

3. Grasp and Grind is   a good employer.
                               a bad employer.
                               about the same as most.

4. The management   deals quickly with employees problems.
                               keeps them waiting.
                               avoids giving an answer.

5. The union   does a good job here.
                                    doesn't seem to do much.
                                    makes more problems than it solves.
6. More shift work is   a good thing.
                                    a bad thing.
                                    bound to come.
7. Everyone knows how the company is doing.
No one knows how the company is doing.
You can find out if you ask.
8. The wage make-up is easy to understand.
                                    difficult and complicated.
                                    understood after the first three or four weeks.
9. Methods of work are badly organized.
                                    very efficient.
                                    good but could be better.

Appendix 5

Example of Formal Communications Structure

DEPARTMENTAL CONSULTATIVE COMMITTEES

The committees will consist of:
The Department Manager (Chairman).
The Department Foreman.
The Area Personnel Officer.
The Senior Department Shop Steward.
An elected shop floor representative.

The committees are advisory. They are intended to exchange information and discuss means of solving problems and improving productivity in the department. The committees will not be directly concerned with negotiations.

The committees will meet monthly and will include a report by the Manager on departmental and company performance and forward programming.

Brief minutes of each meeting will be prepared by the Area Personnel Officer and sent to each committee member and the secretaries of the Main Consultative Committee. A copy of the minutes will also be displayed in the department.

The shop steward member will be the committee's representative on the Main Consultative Committee.

MAIN CONSULTATIVE COMMITTEE

The committee will consist of:
The Plant Director (Chairman).
The Production Manager.
The Personnel Manager.
The Chief Engineer.
Shop Steward representatives from each area committee.
The Chief Shop Steward if he is not a departmental committee representative.
A representative of the non-supervisory staff.

The Personnel Manager and a member elected by the employees' representatives will be joint secretaries of the Committee.

The function of the Committee is broadly:

1. To consider and discuss the present position and future prospects of the company.
2. To consider any matters concerning employment with the company.
3. To examine means of improving the productivity and competitive position of the company.
4. To discuss matters referred by the departmental committees and sub-committees.

Meetings will be held monthly. The agenda for each meeting will be issued by the joint secretaries one week before the meeting. Minutes of each meeting will be prepared by the joint secretaries and circulated to all members within one week of the meeting. Copies will be displayed on all notice boards.

SUB-COMMITTEES

A permanent sub-committee will be the Negotiations Sub-committee. It will consist of the Production Manager, Chief Engineer, Personnel Manager, the Chief Shop Steward and representatives of the main unions.

All negotiations which have not been resolved at departmental level will be referred to this sub-committee. If the sub-committee cannot reach a mutual recommendation to the parties concerned, the matter will be referred to the industry disputes procedure.

I

Appendix 6

Use of Computers in Productivity Bargaining

There are a number of activities involved in or associated with productivity bargaining where computers can make a useful contribution. These have been mentioned, as appropriate, in the text but it is useful to summarize them here.

PRODUCTIVITY MEASUREMENT

The statistical technique of regression analysis is the basic means of establishing relations between input and output, i.e. between floor-to-floor cycle time in work measurement (particularly standard minute regression analysis) and, between total hours and measures of output in productivity measurement. This technique is also useful in job evaluation in establishing the weightings to apply to various factors in factor comparison schemes. The calculations involved in applying these techniques are heavy and difficult and this often imposes a limitation on their use. The computer enables these calculations to be made quickly and with greater precision.

PAIRED COMPARISON IN JOB EVALUATION

This and other consensus methods of job evaluation give rise to a large amount of data which can readily be processed by computer.

SIMULATION OF WAGES STRUCTURE

The problems involved in assessing the cost of a new wages structure compared with an existing one are so complex that it is frequently undertaken as a one-off exercise. Simulation of the existing structure and of possible new structures enables a variety of different propositions to be examined, and a near optimum structure to be determined.

The application of the above techniques depends on the availability of suitable computer programs (soft-ware) together with an understanding of the form in which the information should be prepared for the computer. There are one or two soft-ware houses specializing in this field and reference should be made to the National Computer Centre, Manchester, if it is required to make use of them.

The value of using a computer is that it enables a large variety of solutions to be investigated and hence a better solution should generally be found than by using a manual computation. The costs involved in productivity bargaining are generally so substantial that some effort and cost expended in seeking solutions approaching the best possible should bring a substantial return.

Appendix 7

Guide Lines for Efficiency Agreements including Productivity Agreements

(National Board for Prices and Incomes, Report No. 123 *Productivity Agreements.*)

1st GUIDELINE

It should be shown that the workers are contributing towards the achievement of constantly rising levels of efficiency. Where appropriate, major changes in working practice or working methods should be specified in the agreement.

The objective of efficiency agreements is to make possible the constant raising of efficiency; this will require close and continuing co-operation between managements and workers so as to achieve and maintain the highest standards in the use of both equipment and manpower. The second sentence has special reference to agreements which specify major changes in working practice to which workers have agreed. Such changes should always be spelled out if there is any possibility that commitments in more general terms will lead to difficulties of interpretation or will not be given full expression in practice.

2nd GUIDELINE

Measurements of efficiency should be based on the application of relevant indices of performance or work standards.

Managements should devise and use appropriate yardsticks for measuring the contribution of workers of all kinds towards achieving rising levels of efficiency and develop an information system which makes full use of the data obtained as a result. For many manual operations work-studied standards are applicable and should be used, but work measurement can also be applied to a wide range of clerical and other non-manual work. For other workers in other situations it will be necessary to use more broadly-based indicators of performance, if necessary on a group basis.

3rd GUIDELINE

A realistic calculation of all the relevent costs of the agreement and of the gains attributable to the workers' contribution should normally show that the effect is to reduce the total cost of output or the cost of providing a given service.

'Relevant costs' may include, for example, the cost of redundancy payments or a proportion of consultants' fees where they are an integral part of an agreement, and these should be apportioned as necessary over a reasonable period rather than charged only to the first year following the agreement. The 'gains attributable to the workers' contribution' may result from more effective working methods, the fuller utilization of existing capital equipment, the adaptation of working practices to enable full and prompt use to be made of new equipment and reduce capital investment (if for example revised scheduling and shiftworking make possible a smaller transport fleet). The reference to a reduction in costs assumes a calculation for the purpose of which unrelated costs, e.g., the price of raw materials, are left out of account.

4th GUIDELINE

There should be effective controls to ensure that projected increases in efficiency are achieved and that higher pay or other improvements are made only when such increases are assured

In order to observe this guideline, managements must operate effective controls, including an information system which makes it possible to estimate in advance and subsequently monitor the extent to which increases in efficiency are in fact being achieved. In so far as the information system shows that progress exceeds or falls short of the original projection, some adjustment may need to be made. In any case due allowance should be made for the accrual of some of the achieved gain to the consumer. Particular care also needs to be taken to distinguish the contribution of workers from other sources of more efficient working.

5th GUIDELINE

There should be clear benefits to the consumer by way of a contribution to stable or lower prices.

This guideline is of particular importance in areas of rapid economic expansion, since the most needs to be made of opportunities to reduce prices in these areas in order to contribute as much as possible to raising the real incomes of the community as a whole. In some cases the community may benefit by an improvement in quality while prices remain unchanged or by the use of the gains to compete more effectively in export markets.

6th GUIDELINE

An agreement applying to one group of workers only should bear the cost of consequential increases to other groups, if any have to be granted.

An example would be if supervisors have to be given a pay increase to prevent the disappearance of a differential as a result of a pay increase granted to the workers whom they supervise. The need for consequential increases unrelated to increases in efficiency should, however, be reduced as much as possible by enabling other groups of workers to conclude their own efficiency agreements or by including them within the scope of the original agreement.

7th GUIDELINE

Negotiators should avoid setting levels of pay or conditions which might have undesirable repercussions elsewhere.

Where large increases in pay are shown to be justified negotiators should consider the possibility of staging the increases over a period of time or, alternatively, of a non-recurring lump sum payment. Failure to do so might raise expectations for future increases which could not be fulfilled and might also because of the exceptional size of the increases have repercussions which would eventually rebound on the undertaking granting the original increase.

Bibliography

WORK MEASUREMENT

CURRIE, R. M. (1965). *The measurement of work,* British Institute of Management, London, 416 pp.

DUDLEY, N. A. (1968). *Work measurement—some research studies,* MacMillan, 145 pp.

ABRUZZI, A. (1952). *Work measurement: New Principles and Procedures,* Columbia University Press.

INTERNATIONAL LABOUR OFFICE (1967). *Introduction to Work Study,* I.L.O. Geneva.

WHITMORE, D. A. (1968). *Work Study and related Management Services,* Heinemann.

HEILAND, R. E. and RICHARDSON, W. J. *Work Sampling,* McGraw-Hill.

TIPPETT, L. H. C. (1953). *The ratio delay technique,* Time and Motion Study, May.

MAYNARD, H. B., STEGEMERTEN, G. J. and SCHWAB, J. L. (1948). *Methods-Time Measurement,* McGraw-Hill, New York.

CONSTABLE, J. and SMITH, D. (1966). *Group Assessment Programmes,* Business Publications.

PRODUCTIVITY MEASUREMENT

KENDRICK, J. W. and CRAMER, D. (1965). *Measuring Company Productivity,* The Conference Board, New York.

LYLE, P. (1957). *Regression analysis of Production Costs and Factory Operations,* Oliver and Boyd.

EASTERFIELD, T. E. (1959). *Productivity Measurement in Great Britain,* D.S.I.R., London.

THOMPSON, A. G. (1958). *Productivity Studies and Comparisons in Arc Welding,* Productivity Measurement Review No. 13.

THOMPSON, A. G. (1957). *Measuring and forecasting cost data in highly variable production,* The Institution of Production Engineers Journal, Vol. 36, No. 12.

PRODUCTIVITY IMPROVEMENT

AVERY, M. F. (1962). *Methods Engineering,* McDonald, London.

MILES, L. D. (1961). *Techniques of value analysis and engineering,* McGraw-Hill.

SHAW, A. G. (1952). *The purpose and practice of motion study,* Harlequin Press.

CEMACH, H. P. (1965). *Work Study in the office,* McLaren and Sons.

THOMPSON, A. G. (1968). *A second wind for Cost Reduction,* Financial Times, 6 . 9 . 68

FACTORY. McGraw-Hill Publication, monthly.

ZINCK, W. C. (1962). *Dynamic work simplification,* Reinhold, New York.

WAGES STRUCTURE

B.I.M. *Job Evaluation,* British Institute of Management.

NATIONAL BOARD FOR PRICES AND INCOMES. *Job Evaluation,* Report No. 83, H.M.S.O.

CURRIE, R. M. (1963). *Financial Incentives,* British Institute of Management.

BROWN, W. (1962). *Piecework abandoned,* Heinemann Educational Books.

BENTLEY, F. R. (1964), *People, productivity and progress,* Business Publications.

LESIEUR, F. G. (1968). *The Scanlon plan,* Massachusetts Institute of Technology.

NATIONAL BOARD FOR PRICES AND INCOMES. *Payment by Results,* Report No. 65, H.M.S.O.

PRODUCTIVITY BARGAINING

FLANDERS (1964). *The Fawley Productivity Agreement,* Faber.

NATIONAL BOARD FOR PRICES AND INCOMES. *Productivity Agreements,* Report No. 36, H.M.S.O., Cmnd. 3311.

NATIONAL BOARD FOR PRICES AND INCOMES. *Productivity Agreements,* Report No. 123, H.M.S.O., Cmnd., 4136.

NORTH, D. T. P. and BUCKINGHAM, G. (1969) *Productivity Agreements and Wage Systems,* Gower Press.

TRADES UNION CONGRESS (1966). *Productivity Bargaining.*

McKERSIE, R. B. (1966). *Productivity Bargaining: Deliverance or Delusion,* Personnel Management, September 1966.

THOMPSON, A. G. (1968). How to Productivity Bargain, Personnel, Vol. 1, No. 9.

ROBERTSON, E J. (1968). *Productivity Bargaining and the Engineering Industry,* Enginering Employers' Federation, London.

ALEXANDER, D. C. (Editor) (1969). *A productivity bargaining symposium,* Engineering Employers' Federation, London.

JONES, K. and GOLDING, J. *Productivity Bargaining,* Fabian Research Series, No. 257.

Index

Activity sampling, 19, 22
Added value, 14, 24, 87, 110
  description, 27–28
  monitoring, 106
  relationship to productivity, 28,
    83–84
  Rucker and Scanlon, 59–62
Alcan agreement, 1
Allowances
  conditions, 46, 111
  introductory, 97
  shift, 46, 47, 110, 125
Announcement of proposals, 93–94
Appeals, 84, 90, 113
Arbitration, 79, 96
Attitude surveys, 4, 72–73, 75
  example, 122–125

B.S.I., British Standard Institution
    rating scale, 17–18, 50, 82, 85, 87
Basic rates, see Wage structure
Bedaux plan, 51
Board of Directors, see Management
Bonus schemes, 47–49, 57, 87
  see also Incentives
British Institute of Management, 70
British Oxygen agreement, 1

C.B.I., Confederation of British
    Industry, 77
Capital Investment appraisal, 5, 23
Categories of employees, 11
Change, resistance to, 35, 66–67, 75
Chinese doctor scheme, 57
Classification of grades, 43
Clerical workers
  consultative committee, 99
  measurement and contribution, 11–
    13, 19–22, 31, 103, 119–121
  productivity agreement, 103
Communications and consultation
  attitude surveys, 72

confidential information, 66–67
  departmental, 74
  incentives introduction, 55, 60
  joint consultation, 74–76, 88, 91,
    99, 114–115, 126–127
  management and supervision, 8,
    71, 72, 91–95, 98
  negotiation, fusion with, 76
  negotiators, information for, 66,
    88–89, 95
  preparation of, 75–76, 92
  press, 94, 96
  productivity proposals introduction,
    93–94, 96
  publications and notices, 30, 34, 76,
    93, 96, 100
  sectional agreements, 101
  structure, 99, 107, 114, 126
  union employee channels, 8, 72, 74,
    95
  with D.E.P., 8, 77–78, 90, 96–97,
    101
  employers' associations, 8, 70,
    77–78
  other companies, 94
  union officials, 8, 74, 78, 90, 94–
    95, 96, 101
Community interests, 6
Company policy, related, 90
Computer assistance
  attitude surveys, 72
  job evaluation, 45
  production control, 105
  productivity bargaining, 128–129
  productivity bonus, 97
Consultants, 5, 29, 55, 91
  choice and control, 8, 68–70
Contributions to productivity, 4–7,
    10–40, 105–106
  check lists—labour, 31
  cost reduction, 35–40
  effective time level, 19
  employee, 4, 10–28, 103

Contributions to productivity—contd.
management, 4, 29–40
materials and consumables, 33–34
process elimination, 31
profile of, 12–14, 119–121
staff and service employes, 19–22, 31, 103, 119–121
value analysis, 29, 32, 34
variety reduction, 33
work measurement, 14–22
work simplification, 31
Co-ordinator of productivity bargain, 70, 79, 88–90
Corporate planning, 30, 108
Cost control, 30
Cost reduction, 29, 30, 35–40
analysis of costs, 37–39
participation by employees, 29, 40
potential, 38
responsibility for costs, 40
suggestion schemes, 40
team, 36
Costs and benefits, 5–6, 64, 66, 73, 81, 107

D.E.P., Department of Employment and Productivity, 8, 70, 73, 90, 101
approval, 96–97
assistance, 77–78
Demarcation, 4, 59, 64
see also Flexibility of labour,
Direct workers,
definition, 11
see also Incentives, Work measurement
Discipline, 90, 113
Discounted cash flow, 5
Disputes procedures, 79, 96
Donovan Report, 1
plant/national bargaining, 3
Draft agreement, 88–89

Economics of a company, 10
Element time study, 15
Employers' associations
assistance, 70 77, 78
attitude of, 2, 8, 77
national agreements, 3
Employment policy, 88, 90, 101–102, 115
security, 3, 92

Equal pay, Parkinson Cowan agreement, 117
Expectations and contributions
employees, 3–4, 10–28, 105, 119–121
management, 3–4, 29–40, 119–121

Factor comparison, 43
Fairfields' agreement, 67
Fall-back rates, 46, 109
Fawley agreement, 1, 64
Financial aspects of productivity bargaining, 5–6, 66
costs and benefits, 5, 6, 64, 66, 73, 81, 107
costs categorization, 37–40
discounted cash flow, 5
economics of a company, 10
Flanders, Alan, 1
Flexibility of labour, 4, 54, 59, 64, 98, 108, 112

Geared incentives, 51–53
Grades, 85
Grading, 43
Guide lines for Productivity agreements, 2–3, 130

Halsey plan, 51
Haynes plan, 51
Herzberg, 54
Historical records—productivity, 83

Implementing agreements, 97–100
Implications of productivity bargaining, 7
Incentives
advantages/disadvantages, 56
bonus schemes, 47–49, 57, 87
booking control, 55, 83, 104, 105
Chinese doctor, 57
craft workers, 56
gearing, 51–53
individual/small group, 49–56
interim awards, 97–98
introductory awards, 97–98
large group, 56–57
material usage, 34
measured daywork, 58–59
monitoring, 48, 55, 104–106
penalty schemes, 57

Incentives—contd.
performance, 10, 18, 50–62, 81–83, 104–106
proportional, 51
Rowan plan, 51
Rucker and Scanlon plans, 59–62
sub-standard work, 56, 110
survey of schemes, 82–83
waiting time, 48, 54
see also Work measurement
Incomes policy, 63
Indirect workers
definition, 11
see also Incentives, Work measurement
Industrial engineering department, 68, 69, 79
see also Work Study department
Industrial relations
case law, 106, 107
Donovan Report, 3
incentives, effect, 47–48, 54, 59
policies, 54, 108
productivity bargaining, effect, 9, 66, 93, 95, 100, 104, 107–108
Inflation, 6
Information, *see* Communications and consultation
Interim awards, 4, 5, 97–98, 116

Job enlargement, *see* Flexibility of labour
Job evaluation
administration, 69, 84
committee, 84
computer assistance, 45
employee administered, 116
factor comparison, 43
grading, 43
job descriptions, 41
paired comparisons, 44
points rating, 44
ranking, 42
relation to wage structure, 84, 86
statistical techniques, 45
training for, 42
Joint consultation, 74–76, 88, 91
Joint development of proposals, 90–91
Joint union committee, 79

Key men—retention of, 71

Labour—*see* Manning
Labour cost, 24, 27–28, 35, 59–62, 66
see also Added value
Labour turnover, 84, 97
Long-range planning, 7, 108

M.T.M., Motion Time Measurement, 21
Management
Board involvement, 8, 65–71, 98, 101
communications, 8, 71–72, 91–95, 98
continuity, 8, 99
contributions to productivity, 11–14, 29–40, 119–121
line involvement, 8, 71–75, 84, 91, 93, 94, 95
preparation of, 65–73
resources, 66–68, 101
retention of key members, 71
survey of views, 4, 72, 122–123
Management Services department, 66–67
Manning
reduction, 5, 29, 35, 101, 103
redundancy policy, 90, 101, 115
supply, 5, 7, 64, 84, 97, 108
Maintenance
control, 30, 66
incentives, 56, 57, 87
labour, 11, 19, 22, 38, 39, 82, 113, 119
Materials, 7, 8, 10, 28, 33, 34, 35
Measured daywork, 58–59
Measurement, productivity, *see* Productivity measurement
work, *see* Work measurement
Method study, 29–34
Mobility of labour, 4, 54, 59, 64, 108, 112
Monitoring results, 9, 15, 40, 67, 104–108
Motivation, 9, 44–62, 108

National agreements, 3, 77
National Board for Prices and Incomes, 1, 54, 77, 96
guide lines for agreements, 2, 130

National Computer Centre, 128
Negotiations, 5, 9
  case law, 106-107
  committee, 79, 91, 92
  conduct of, 89, 95-96
  effect of district committees, 90
  fusion with consultation, 76, 91
  information supporting, 66, 88-89, 95
  staff workers, 103
  system, 78-79, 114
  union ability, 74

O. & M., Organization and Methods, 29
Objectives of productivity bargaining, 7
Outline productivity agreement, 81-84
Output/input relationship, 22-27,
  see also Productivity measurement
Overtime, 5, 6, 24, 47, 102

P.M.T.S., Pre-determined Motion Time Systems, 20
Paired comparisons, 44
Parkinson Cowan agreement, 116-117
Participative proposal forming, 90-91
Payment by results, see Incentives
Performance—definition, 18,
  see also Work measurement
Personnel department, 8, 66-67, 79, 84, 126
  calibre, 68
  setting-up, 68-69
Pilot schemes, 96
Points rating, 44
Preparations for productivity bargaining
  check list, 80
  communications, 75-76, 92
  D.E.P., 77-78
  employees, 73-75
  employers' associations, 77
  line management/supervision, 71-73
  management resources, 66-68
  negotiating system, 79-80
  outline agreement, 81-84
  press statements, 94, 96
  shop stewards, 73-74

statement of intent, 91-93
top management, 65-71
union officials, 78
wages structure, 81, 84-87
Pressures for productivity bargaining, 63-65
Process elimination, 31
Production control and planning, 20, 30, 48, 105
Production values, see Added value
Productivity agreements
  Alcan Industries, 1
  British Oxygen, 1
  Esso, Fawley, 1, 64
  Fairfields', 67
  Parkinson Cowan, 116-118
  Rootes, Linwood, 1
  Tubes Limited, 2, 109-116
Productivity measurement, 5
  activity sampling, 19, 22
  added value relationship, 28
  categories of employees, 11
  computer assistance, 128
  control chart, 26
  economics of a company, 10
  labour hours, estimated, 25
  large groups, 15, 22-23
  methodology, 25-27
  mix effect, 23, 24, 26
  monitoring, 106
  output/input ratio, 22-27
  preliminary assessment, 83
  profile of contributions, 12-14
  scheduling, 20
  small groups, 14-15
  staff workers, 11-13, 19-22, 31, 119-121
  varying factors, 23-24
  volume effect, 25
  work-in-progress, 26
Profit sharing, 7, 27
Profits—information, 66-67
Protection of earnings, 49, 97, 111, 117
Publicity, external, 94, 96
  internal, 30, 34, 76, 93, 96, 100
Purchasing, 33-34

Quality, 10, 29, 56, 110
Quality control, 26, 30-31, 34, 48

Ranking, 42
Rates of pay, *see* Wage structure
Recruitment, *see* Manning
Redundancy policy, 90, 101, 115
Representation of employees, 40, 73–74, 84, 95, 99, 125
Restrictive practices, 4, 64
  see also Flexibility of labour
Review of agreement, *see* Monitoring results
Rootes, Linwood agreement, 1
Rowan plan, 51
Royal Commission on Trade Unions and Employers' Associations, *see* Donovan Report

Sales
  deliveries, 7, 66
  potential, 5, 33, 66, 100, 107
  prices, 6, 107
Scanlon plan, 61–62
Scheduling, 20
Sectional agreements, 7, 100–101, 103
Security of employment, 3, 92
  policy, 88, 90, 101–102, 115
Service labour, 11, 19, 22, 38, 39, 113, 119
Share of benefits, 6, 60, 107
Shiftwork, 4, 5, 93
  payment, 46–47, 110, 125
Shop stewards, *see* Trade unions
Skilled workers, 11, 19, 22, 28, 39, 43, 82, 113, 119
  incentives, 56–57, 87
Specialist staff, 67–68, 88
Staff workers
  consultative representation, 99
  measurement and contributions, 11–13, 19–22, 31, 119–121
  separate agreement, 103
Standard minutes, 17–18, 25, 83
Standard minute regression analysis, 18–19
Standardization, 33
Statement of intent, 9, 91–93
Storage, 31–32
Strikes—record, 9
Suggestion Schemes, 40, 58
Supervisors
  communications with, 8, 71–73, 91, 93–95, 99

contribution, 11–14, 19, 119–121
preparation, 69, 71–73, 98
role, 8, 14, 35, 40, 58, 73, 95, 98–99, 119–121
salaries, 5, 73, 98, 103–104
survey of views, 72
Survey of incentives, 82–83
Survey of attitudes, 72–73, 75, 122–125
Synthetic values, 15

Tea breaks, 113
Timekeeping and attendance, 4, 84, 113
Timetable
  consultants, 69
  overall, 4, 65, 67–68, 79–80, 93, 102–103
  work measurement, 97, 103
Trade Unions
  absence of, 74
  communication channels, 8, 72, 74, 95
  craft attitudes, 56
  district committees, 89–90
  effective representation, 73–74, 95, 125
  local officials, 8, 74, 78, 90, 94–96, 101
  multi-union situations, 79, 95–96
  national bargaining, 3, 77
  shop stewards, 8, 9, 23, 66–67, 72–74, 76, 78, 84, 89, 91, 94–96, 101, 103, 116, 123, 126–127
  staff unions, 98, 103
Training, 54, 70
  allowances, 110
  co-ordinator, 70
  incentive introduction, 55
  job evaluation, 42
  management and supervision, 69, 72, 98, 103
  shop stewards, 69, 74, 103
Transfers, 111
Tubes Limited agreement, 1, 109–116

Unit costs, 8, 34
U.S. workers—comparison, 1

Value analysis, 29, 32–34

Variety reduction, 33
Volume of production, 5

Wage structures, 3–5, 46–69, 64, 84,
   109
  analysis, 81–84
  base rates, 46, 109
  computer assistance, 85, 128
  development, 9, 46, 84–87
  earnings stability, 48–49, 56, 110–
   111
  grade division, 85
  incentives, *see* Incentives
  job evaluation, 41–46, 81, 84–86
  overtime/shift pay, 47, 110, 125
  sectional awards, 101
  simulation of, 85, 128
Waiting time, 30, 54, 111
Work factor, 21
Work-in-progress, 23, 26, 106
Work measurement, 5, 10–28
  B.S.I., British Standard Institution
   rating scale, 17–18, 50, 82, 85,
   87
  M.T.M., Motion Time Measurement, 20

P.M.T.S., Pre-determined Motion
  Time Study, 20
  activity sampling, 19, 22
  bench marks, 20
  contingencies, 17
  element time study, 15
  estimated times, 20
  individual/small group, 14, 49–56
  large group, 56–62
  monitoring, 104–106
  performance, 10, 18, 50–62, 81–83,
   104–106
  rating, 15–16
  rest allowances, 17
  standard data, 21
  standard minutes, 17–18, 25, 83
  standard times, 17
  timetable, 97, 103
  waiting time, 30, 54, 111
Work simplification, 29, 31–32
Work Study department, 8, 55–56, 84
  calibre, 68
  setting-up, 68–69

Yield (material), 7, 8, 10, 11, 33–35